YOU GOT THIS!

YOU GOT THIS!

How to Fulfill Your God-given Dreams & Visions

FELICIA ASOMANING

Destiria Inc.

Copyright © 2021 by Felicia Asomaning

All rights reserved solely by the author. The author guarantees all contents are original and do not infringe upon the legal rights of any other person or work. No part of this book may be reproduced in any form without the permission of the author. The views expressed in this book are not necessarily those of the publisher.

Unless otherwise indicated, Scripture quotations taken from the King James Version (KJV) – *public domain*.

Scripture quotations taken from the Amplified Bible (AMP). Copyright © 1954, 1958, 1962, 1964, 1965, 1987 by The Lockman Foundation. Used by permission. All rights reserved.

Printed in the United States of America.

I dedicate this book to the memory of my father, the late **Reynolds Asomaning**, *the Revolutionist.*
Daddy, your legacy lives on!

Acknowledgements

I am not self-made. From my conception to my becoming, there have always been people who have contributed to my life and well being:

To my Heavenly Father who formed me in my mother's womb and breathed life into me, I am the embodiment of your Divine Thoughts. Thank you for giving me expression in this world. To the Lover of my soul, Jesus Christ who continues to give me infinite reasons to love Him, thank you for dying and securing a pleasurable place in You for me. To my Best Friend and Greatest Helper, who literally kept me on my toes to pen down the revelation He downloaded into my spirit and helped me through the entire process, The Precious Holy Spirit. I owe you my life. Use me God for your Glory!

To the first woman who felt my heartbeat, carried and nurtured me before the world met me- MOM, this is for you! Thank you for your endless sacrifices and continual support throughout the years. I can never repay you for all that you do for me. May the Lord reward you immensely.

To the Asomaning Family, thank you for your unconditional love and support throughout the years. We are in this journey together.

To Apostle Reindorf and Pastor Pamela Mantey, thank you for investing in my life.

To Apostle George Tetteh, this is the fruit of your seeds of encouragement. You were the first to see the writing potential in me and encouraged me to perfect my craft because it is a "weapon."

Anyone who holds this book in their hands is blessed because of you.

To Pastor Margaret Agyapong, thank you for everything you do for me.

To Apostle Stephen Chestnut, thank you for believing in me and encouraging me to soar.

To Mother Josephine Manuel, your daily intercession and encouragement has fostered my healing and this book is proof of a healed heart. Thank you.

To my Unplugged Nation, thank you for your support and trusting me to be your Pastor.

Finally to my remaining squad, too many to name here, I'm grateful for all of you. Thank you for everything.

NOW it's YOUR — TIME —

Introduction

Whew!
What a year 2020 has been! It's difficult to avoid the cliché: we slept in one world and woke up in another. And if you are like me, you probably started the year with high hopes, making great resolutions and claiming "Vision 2020!"

Then suddenly, Covid-19 showed up and turned the whole world upside down! A thousand dreams became mission impossible. We witnessed the horrifying scenes of precious lives taken away by this deadly virus and the damaging effects it also brought.

Suddenly, the whole world seemed to have been paused as humanity tried to navigate the global crisis that affected the world economy and way of living. For the first time, nations were on lockdowns, companies were shut down, some businesses even collapsed, and several jobs were lost.

Subsequently, people's hopes were dashed, and many are still confused and frustrated. All over the world, families are trying to make ends meet, heal from the grief or trauma of their losses, and rebuild their lives without their loved ones. It was becoming clear that the world we knew pre-Covid-19 was gone, and we may need to brace ourselves to face a new world. It is now a world that rips off control and influence in the systems we have grown accustomed to—leaving many with deep-seated fear and vulnerability.

However, what if life was never about control but courage? What if it is not about getting but releasing? What if the pandemic came to reveal the resilience of the human spirit? What if the perfect vision we claimed as our mantra and resolutions was actually possible, and this storm is actually clearing our path?

In a world filled with questions, I sense a divine urgency to release hope for navigating life after spells of disappointment and discouragement. As we tiptoed into another year, you may wonder and ask yourself a bunch of questions: *where is hope for 2021 and beyond? How can I create beauty from ashes? Where is God in the middle of this? Does He even care? If He does, what plans does He have for me? Where can I find the strength to love life, dream again, and live well?*

My heart goes to anyone who feels the world's weight on their shoulders, people who are unsettled with the uncertainties of their present conditions and crying through the pain. I also feel for those grieving their loss and afraid in a post-pandemic world. I understand because we are in this together.

Nevertheless, I pray you never lose hope because there is a God who still makes beautiful dreams happen. He wants you and me to dream again. This is His gift to you—a blueprint for changing your life by finding and living out His divine purpose for your life. Don't despair about the new normal. We were not made for the *new* or *old* NORMAL! We were created to alter the status quo. We were not designed to wait for the future but to strive today to create one. Actually, we were created to thrive in every season of life.

I'm about to speak passion and inspiration back into your world to propel you from the place of trials into your testimonies. I want to equip you with success hacks and mind tools to help you find long-term fulfillment and success under any climate.

Wherever you are right now in your journey, I need you to understand that you are not alone. You are reading this line because you made it! And you can have hope for the future because God believes in you—you got this!

So, what do you do when you come under mountain-high rubble of uncertainty, fear, unresolved past, and people's expectation?

Where can you find the faith to face your giants? How can you draw strength to leap over heights that stopped people who seem better than you? Do you feel overwhelmed and out of sync with your true self? Then, it might be a good time to expect help from a greater source.

My Story

One way to trust God in this age is to look back and see what He has done in ages past. We need a reference for faith, and we need faith for decisive actions. When we examine the paths that brought us from where we were to days of better testimonies, we are encouraged to face the future with confidence.

My story is no different. I have experienced God's intervention time and time again. One particular account has to do with my journey to self-discovery. You know you need God's intervention when your college career advisor has a candid conversation with you and says, *"Felicia, it's time to decide what you're going to do with your life. You can't keep switching your majors around, hopping from one to another and dropping two weeks after. You've got to decide on something and stick to it!"* I experienced dark moments in the maze of life. With tears streaming down my face, I knew she was right. I could not be an undeclared major forever, but she did not realize that the answer was not an easy one. In fact, it was the beginning of a journey that would require me to have an honest assessment of my life which eventually would lead to my decision to drop out of college for a season.

Growing up, I was not like most young adults who seem to know exactly what they want to do with their lives after high school. Actually, mine was an interesting experience. I immigrated from Ghana,

West Africa, to join my mother in the United States in my early teens. As expected, I experienced culture shock while adapting to my new world.

However, my academic achievements would soon cover up my insecurities as my family and loved ones watched me excel in my academics. It would not take long for me to be recognized as a "brainiac" in class by my colleagues, with my lowest score being A-.

By my junior year in high school, it was becoming clear that I was marked for success with an impressive 3.9 GPA. I made my family proud with my academic achievements, and those around me saw my potential for greatness. Yet, I struggled secretly, and my quest for discovering my purpose and identity continued into my college years.

My struggles wore me out, and with time, misery and depression took over. Although I loved the Lord and I have been rooted in church since infancy, I just could not navigate my way through the pressure of impressing my family who had their own expectation of me living the American Dream.

As a child of an immigrant, my life was not fully my own in my African household. I had to literally realize the desires of a single mother who had also charted a path for her only child. There was no room for failure or mistakes. As I watched them plan my future, no one ever consulted God about any of those plans. However, it would not take long for Him to prove that He is the One who is really in charge, and He did have plans which were contrary to their expectations yet bigger and even better.

MY EPIPHANY

While it is understandably difficult to make sense of sorrow and pain, I believe that we can maximize our gains even in pain by listening to the inner voice that is being drowned in the noise of everyday life. For me, an epiphany meant I could no longer define success from the content of other people's dictionaries. I knew it was time to come out of that prison if I really wanted to be authentically me, and that would mean it was time to let go of trying to live up to other people's expectations of me. It was time to find my path and live out God's dreams for my life, despite not knowing how to realize them.

On life's stormy sea, I found a guiding star, a light within that set me on a life-changing journey. What did I do and get? I made a decision and literally witnessed my evolution. This book is a byproduct of that. It is almost two decades since my epiphany, yet I'm still evolving, working, and realizing my dreams! I invite you to join me in this experience. You can turn the light on over that situation! You have what it takes to walk into freedom.

What's your story?

Everyone has a story, and yours may be different from mine, and you may currently be on a quest to discover your path to greatness but even if your dreams seem dashed, the fact that you have this book in your hand indicates that you believe there has to be more for you. That alone, my friend, is enough to get you started on your journey to new beginnings. Dream again!

You may have received dreams and visions from God. You might even be moving towards it, but you still doubt His promise because the process is not encouraging. It is perfectly normal to dawdle in the dark, not seeing the end from the beginning—how it is all going to come together. Maybe you feel God's plan is unfolding at snail-speed. Well, stay in that pace!

It is okay to feel tired sometimes, but you cannot stop or turn away from your destiny. You are currently in a place where you are now, trying to defy the odds, launching to leap over institutionalized limitations, fighting to break generational curses, and daring to achieve your dream one step at a time.

Do not despair! This place, time, and season in your life may feel like birth pangs, but it will surely birth your glorious testimony. Your pain has an assignment, and it is working for your good. There is no place for candle lights under the sun, but the nights offer every candle a chance to glow. Likewise, your night season is only offering an opportunity for your light to shine.

Perhaps you feel like you're on the other side of the world and wallowing in confusion, wondering what on earth you are here for. Whatever stage of life you find yourself in, I have great news for you: *God has good plans for your life, and if you cooperate with Him, all things are possible!*

The Big Picture: You were born to be Great!

You and I were born to make a difference, and the drive to act will never stop until you have realized the aspirations that are submerged in the fiber of your being.

I believe there is greatness inside of you, and that is the reason I wrote this book!

I know how it feels to be stranded and confused, not knowing which step to take in my life, but I'm at peace, knowing that I have a Big God who gave me Big Dreams. Today, I am helping other people realize their God-given dreams! That, my friend, is a living and faithful testimony of the goodness of God: that He has incredible plans up His sleeves concerning you.

WHAT TO EXPECT

While there is no singular way to fulfill your God-given dreams, I believe the principles God used for Jesus' birth and the fulfillment of His purpose in only three and a half years are worthy of emulation. Now, this does not mean we will live for only three and half years, but those principles are timeless, and if God used them to work out His plans for Jesus, they would also work for you.

I believe God has allowed me to write this book to reinforce spiritual truths that can only be found in His Word. Therefore, I can confidently say that if you follow the principles within this book, you are guaranteed good success in your God-given endeavors. You will thrive in your purpose while enjoying a deep and intimate relationship with Jesus Christ.

In this book, you will learn what to do when you receive dreams from God: conceiving, birthing, protecting, and nurturing them until they can outlive you—creating a trans-generational impact that cannot be erased from the sands of time. This is what I believe purposeful living is about; anything outside of that is not what God intended for you.

So, whether you are seventeen years old or now starting life afresh or in your seventies thinking life is over, I pray that as you read this book, the Holy Spirit will use it to illuminate your vision. He will give you the clarity you need and enable you to step confidently into your mandate.

If you are ready to walk in your greatness and maximize your potential, hop in because, *honey, you are in for a fantastic adventure with God!*

> "Consult not your fears but your hopes and your dreams. Think not about your frustrations but about your unfulfilled potential. Concern yourself not with what you tried and failed in, but with what is still possible for you to do."
>
> —POPE JOHN PAUL XXIII[1]

Your Destiny Cheerer,
Felicia.

Contents

Dedication	v
Acknowledgements	vii
Photo Insert	ix
Introduction	x
Photo Insert	1
SECTION I	2
1 Defining Your Moments	3
2 Why Not You?	13
3 You Are God's Wildest Dream	24
4 Dream and Vision Expressions	35
5 What the Heck Am I Doing?	46
6 Mission Possible	66
Photo Insert	75
SECTION II	76
7 God's Got You	77
8 Embracing Your Mentors	96
9 Your Silent Heroes	105
10 Embracing Your Tribe	121
Photo Insert	132

SECTION III		133
11 The Secret to Long Term Success		134
Photo Insert		148
SECTION IV		149
12 The Assassin Of Your Dreams		150
Photo Insert		180
SECTION V		181
13 Your Passport to Possibilities		182
Photo Insert		190
Knowing Jesus Intimately		191
Work With Me		193
Photo Insert		194
Meet the Author		195
End Notes		196

SECTION I

Unwrapping #YourSwag

Welcome to the first section of this book. This is the part where we unwrap the gift of You! That's right, You as the Person you were born to be; the masterpiece of God's fine art and the embodiment of His Divine thoughts.

In this section, you will be introduced to the real You through the lens of your Creator. Who is better to tell you about the potentials of a creation than the Creator? As you read this book, you will encounter your uniqueness and discover what makes you special. You will be challenged to put down all the lies you've been told and all the limiting beliefs you have held, and you will be encouraged to embrace an achiever who can change the world by means of a serious Partnership with their Creator and by embracing the assignments He has for you.

So, get yourself ready because we are going in for the full unveiling of awesome wonder, wrapped in a delicate and fine human vessel. Let's get to it!

1

Defining Your Moments

> *"It's not what happens in our life that defines us, rather it is how we respond to what happens in our life that really defines who we are."*
>
> -BRANDON HARRISON²

She was America's home management Queen! The home was her throne and the media her empire. From writing books, publishing magazines, gardening, folding sheets, baking the best cookies, cleaning the home, and showing how to throw the best events and entertaining guests with class, she wowed her viewers who became loyal clients of her homemaking skills and subsequently, rewarding her for that, making her the first female self-made billionaire in the United States.

However, 2004 saw her domestic media and business empire crumbling down as she faced indictment for insider trading in which she was found guilty of conspiracy, obstruction of justice, and lying to federal investigators about a stock sale.

Clearly, it was a defining moment that would interrupt her business empire and cause her to face jail time. Yet, this was a moment in time that would alter her life forever and would position her for a new discovery that would produce growth and evolution.

She served five months in a federal correctional facility following her conviction and another six months under house arrest. But, if Charles R. Swindoll's statement is true that "life is ten percent what happens to you and ninety percent how you react to it,"[3] then Martha Stewart, the Domestic Diva, really proved her queendom that truly you can resurrect out of anything that life throws at you. Because she came out of jail and took ownership of her influence, rebuilt her company, and doubled what she originally made prior to her jail experience. She defined the moments that were thrown at her, by making lemonade from the lemons and thriving on the steps of her shame to massive success. Today she has become an inspiration to many.[4]

Life is full of moments that define us: some good, some bad, and some so ugly we choose not to remember. But it is through these defining moments that our lives are shaped as our reality is changed and we are redefined. These moments can either be positive or negative, depending on how they are interpreted through our lens. These are what we call defining moments!

A defining moment is simply anytime in your life in which a choice that you make or an incident that happens causes a change in your life—a moment in time that defines your life.

As humans, we will have many of these moments in our lives: being born as infants, learning to walk, stepping into adolescence, graduating from high school, going to college, getting married, being a parent for the first time, experiencing the death of a loved one among others.

As a Christian you also have many defining moments in your walk with God. From the day you gave your life to Christ, to your experience with the baptism of the Holy Spirit to your first trial to weathering a major storm in your life, your life will see many defining moments that can be channeled as stepping stones to your progress in the pursuit of your God-given mandate.

Thankfully, Martha Stewart was able to come back and regain her business empire. But what happens when you are not awarded the opportunity to serve jail time and return? What happens when it seems life has come to a halt for you and you are now forced to run for your life because you are now the most wanted, with your name in the tabloids and in the media? At worst, the leader of the land himself is looking for you? Such was the situation of Moses, God's ideal and preferred candidate to use as a mighty deliverer of the Jewish people from their Egyptian bondage.

Bravo, God!

> *How are you responding to the turn of events in your life?*

The difference between Martha Stewart and Moses is that while they lived in two different time zones, countries, and backgrounds they both committed a crime, they both came back to the very "place" where they previous reigned, one by choice and the other by divine commission. Nevertheless, they were both given another chance to pursue their innate dreams. This is to make you also feel that no matter where you're from, whether from a prestige background or you currently find yourself at the backside of the desert, God sees you!

So, permit me to dive in to the dynamic and complex life and legacy of a man whose trajectory of life would not only alter his life but the destiny of an entire nation—Moses!

We are introduced to him right from the second chapter of Exodus, a book that he wrote, and almost the entire book is centered on him, his genesis, his calling to leadership, and the birth and establishment of Israel as a new nation. Actually, his life was full of many dramatic defining moments that are worth highlighting. Here is a brief outline of those defining moments in his life:

- He was born to a Hebrew slave parents,
- He was the last born of three children.
- At the time of his birth, there was a law already in effect in the whole of Egypt, issued by the Pharaoh, that all male newborn babies should be killed, but his mother hid him for three months
- He was put in the Nile river with his sister keeping watch.
- He was taken from the water and adopted by the Pharaoh's daughter
- He was then raised and weaned by his biological mother.
- Then he was adopted and raised in the Palace as Prince.
- As a young man, he had an "urge" to check on his Hebrew brethren and ended up killing a cruel Egyptian taskmaster who apparently was fighting with a Jew.
- He became a runaway convict who fled to the wilderness and settled there.
- He was married to a daughter of a priest and started a family.
- He became a shepherd and stayed in Midian for forty years.
- God called him in his 80s and commissioned him to deliver His people from bondage.
- He returned to Egypt and confronted Pharaoh, backed with ten plagues sent by his God until his people were finally released.
- He crossed the Red Sea with the Israelites and led them into the wilderness.

- He established the constitution and government structure of a new nation.
- He stayed with the people in the wilderness until he died at the age of 120 years.

Bewildering, huh? Well, as you can see, there were many dynamics to his complex upbringing and to the mandate placed upon his life. It seems as if the first eighty years of his life were evolution and preparation for the second phase, which was the actual response to the mandate.

Permit me to dig deeper.

First of all, the name Moses, is a Hebrew verb which means "to pull out/draw out" [of water], and the infant Moses was given this name by Pharaoh's daughter after rescuing him from the Nile (Ex. 2:10).

His very first identity by the Egyptians was the fact of his background, and he would later be identified by them as a murderer. By calling him daily as Moses, he was constantly reminded of his history.

Do you find yourself being defined by your background—gender, race, socio-economic status, mistakes, ethnicity, religious or political affiliations? Such was the dilemma of Moses.

Now, let's go further:

There are three categories of people we can derive from Moses's life:

HIS INFANCY TO FORTY YEARS: THE YOUNG EGYPTIAN PRINCE.

After Moses was adopted by Pharaoh's daughter, he basically received all the privileges of being raised as a royal. He was an Egyptian prince in a time when Egypt was a superpower nation. Pharaoh was considered to be a god and people worshiped him. Thus, as a potential Pharaoh, Moses had the whole world at his disposal. Also, he was intelligent, educated, and had the strength and vigor of a young man—the epitome of power.

In application, the young Moses represents the young person with dreams and a brilliant future glaring in their face. If you are in this season, you are afforded the opportunity to maximize your time and moments and step straight into God's purpose for you, with the right guidance and without all those costly mistakes of your older counterparts.

The future looks bright and promising. You may not fully know where you are heading but you are confident about what lies ahead of you. You have strength and vigor and youthful advantage above your older counterparts.

You are encouraged to dream big and go after your heart's desires. Many people excuse your adventurous prowess with a nodded yes because they expect you to explore. And, depending on your circumstances, you may or may not have minimal responsibilities. This is also the stage when many young people start to settle down and begin their families, their careers, and laying the groundwork for their futures.

FROM FORTY YEARS TO EIGHTY YEARS: THE MIDDLE-AGED RUNAWAY CONVICT, FAMILY MAN, AND A SHEPHERD.

In this phase, Moses experienced more defining moments from becoming a husband, a father, and a shepherd. It was in this phase that he was actually groomed and trained by his father-in-law in his priestly responsibilities, his fathering responsibilities through the raising of his biological children, and also in his leadership responsibilities through his marriage as a husband and also as a shepherd of his family's flock through providence.

If you are in this stage of life, you have probably had your own share of defining moments—from being a parent to growing in your career to being established in life—many of us are not afforded the privilege of being so adventurous as our younger counterparts as the responsibilities of our stages gives us limited access, yet we can capitalize those moments to achieve our dreams.

FROM 80 TO 120 YEARS OF AGE: THE SENIOR CITIZEN WHO WOULD SOON ENCOUNTER GOD AND RECEIVE HIS MANDATE TO FREE GOD'S PEOPLE FROM THEIR EGYPTIAN OPPRESSION AND LAY DOWN THE FOUNDATION OF A NEW NATION.

This phase in Moses's life was the most pivotal; it was the phase during which he officially received his mandate from God to deliver the Israelites from the very place he'd fled and lay the groundwork to birth a new nation. Most people in our modern times would count people in this age group in retirement mode. Meaning, you are either on a paid pension, in a nursing home, or not too active in making major decisions or growing careers. In fact, you are considered a senior citizen, recounting the past and depending on the quality of life lived, maybe living in regrets or fulfillment.

This is also the phase in which our physical strength fails us, our beauty fades, and there are visible signs of aging with corresponding pains and physical ailments that require constant medical attention and monitoring.

However, if God could find Moses relevant despite the younger people in Israel, then I put it to you that you can allow God to use any age in your life to define the seed of greatness He has invested in you to benefit the destiny of others around you.

Moses's dream of being a deliverer was never dashed before God, because He was the source of it. While life's hard experiences may have beaten him down, they were actually preparing Moses for the work God had for him. Probably he felt grateful and content to have been given a second chance to rebuild another life for himself, after the spectacles of Egypt as a fallen prince, who knows he might have been dead. But here he stood, having attained a normal life of what was considered a "successful man" by the standards of his time—married with children in a stable and safe life, staying out of trouble.

Yet destiny was about to call and it would interrupt the trajectory of his life again—this time taking him to the very place he dreaded never to see again and with a dream that almost got him killed, now becoming a vision to be realized—in his old age, and this time with clarity of purpose and an endorsement of a covenant keeping God.

Reading this, you will soon discover that your life fits in one of the three stages of Moses's life. Maybe all of us can identify with Moses because his life represents the life experiences that shape and define us into the purpose God has for us. Life is a delivery room that is constantly drawing things of us—our potential—that we didn't know existed through the defining moments that are presented to us, and should we capitalize on those moments, we can literally soar into our dreams and visions despite the obstacles that seem to threaten us. The good news is that, no matter the stage you are in today, the world is still before you to conquer.

One of the key principles of Moses's life is that you can't blow out God's dreams for your life. In fact, at every stage, experiences and even the mistakes were all part of God's plan to conform Moses to the purpose of His will for his life and the corporate purpose of the children of Israel.

Every experience was necessary and each phase vital. Should Moses had skipped the desert experience, he would have been robbed of his keen "shepherd" skills, priest training from his father in law, and the skills of a husband and a father that are all necessary life skills needed to be an effective leader in governing the new nation for forty years.

Hence, don't resent your moments—the ones that stretch you the most and refine your character and cause you to grow. Your defining moments prepare you and also build the platform(s) to launch and realize your dreams and visions.

I once found a quote on social media by Lisa Bevere which said, "*If you think you have blown God's plan for you, think again because you are not that smart.*"[5]

Indeed, Moses soon discovered the reality that he may have run away from the Egyptians but not away from God; His plans for him were still right on schedule.

Do You Feel You Rushed Ahead of God's Timing?

You might be feeling less than important with your dreams and hopes dashed or you are in the prime of your youth, with future golden, this is for you too. You may be an empty nester and think life is over for you because you are older and probably missed the opportunities or have been eating the consequences of bad decisions. Guess what: God still sees you and He is still counting on you.

Those mistakes can be used by God to birth miracles in another generation. Needless to say, what He has for you is still for you!

As long as there is breath in you, God is not through with you. Moses was only getting started at eighty years of age! His desire to deliver his people from bondage was about to get clearer now than ever in his life. It is also important to note that when God commissioned Moses, He never discussed his past mistakes or crime.

Likewise, God is not counting your wrongs. He has no business in that. No matter what stage you are in life, you can allow God to help you translate the defining moments in your life to birth and realize the dreams and visions He gave you to fulfill your purpose.

Allow God to define your moments and interpret them through the lens of His purpose for your life to maximize every given moment. Let Him draw the treasures, the lessons and your evolution from them to help you accomplish His purpose for your life.

> "In Him also we have obtained an inheritance, being predestined according to the purpose of Him who works all things according to the counsel of His will"
>
> **(EPH. 1:11 NKJV).**

KEY TAKEAWAY: We are truly defined by the series of moments that alter our lives forever. We call them defining moments. Don't be afraid to embrace your journey, capitalizing on those moments to your advantage.

2

Why Not You?

"But [a]when she saw him, she was troubled at his saying, and considered what manner of greeting this was. Then the angel said to her, 'Do not be afraid, Mary, for you have found favor with God'"

(LUKE 1:29-30 NKJV).

The angel Gabriel was sent by God to go into a city in Galilee named Nazareth, to appear to a young virgin who was engaged to a man and minding her own business, to get her to go into some kind of contract where God was going to borrow her womb to birth the Second Person of the Trinity, Jesus Christ, who would save the world from sin.

According to ancient prophecies, God had promised the coming of the Messiah, a savior who would finally rescue Israel from their oppressive leaders and reconcile the entire human race back to the Heavenly Father's arms. For 400 years, it seemed as if the promise of God was never going to be fulfilled, and the hopes of God's chosen people were dashed over and over, as many generations rose and died with no savior in sight. However, God is always faithful to His promises; He knew the appointed time when He would send His Son to the earth.

Apparently, to fulfill prophecy, the Messiah was to be the fruit of the woman who, according to Genesis 3:15, would crush the serpent's head while he bruises his heel. He was to be born of a virgin (Isa. 7:14) and would spring from the root of David (Isa. 11:1–2; Rev. 5:5; 22:16). God was very precise that the Messiah would be a Nazarene (Isa. 11:1; 53:3; Ps. 22).

Ever been in a situation where you felt unqualified for the task at hand and at worst found yourself looking down on yourself because you were scared to death about the assignment or probably felt intimidated by those who considered themselves "gurus" or "pros" and you felt like a little ant amongst them?

Well, Mary, the soon to be mother of Jesus, didn't consider herself to be the ideal candidate to be chosen to birth and raise the Son of God on earth. So, it would make perfect sense to feel confused and disturbed about the greeting which sounded so strange to her coming from an angel. I know I would but that is also the beautiful thing about the goodness of God: He chooses us not because we think we deserve it or we even qualify for it but because He is good! What God was about to do through Mary had nothing to do with her but more with who He is and His love for humanity.

Therefore, what Mary was experiencing here was a glimpse of what the grace of God feels like. When we receive the unmerited favor of God, it's because He chooses to bestow it upon us not virtue of our own works. Mary had found favor with God, so she was blessed and highly favored "among" other women.

Do you know that you also have been found worthy to birth those dreams and visions God has impregnated in you by His Spirit? Contrary to people's negative opinions or even your own negative self-talks, God begs to differ!

Mary had found favor with God and so have you.

God Doesn't Make Junk!

I once heard a story of a woodcutter who one day took his grandson into the forest for his first experience in selecting and cutting oak trees. These they would later sell to the boat builders. As they walked along, the woodcutter explained that the purpose of each tree is contained in its natural shape: some are straight for planks, some have the proper curves for the ribs of a boat, and some are tall for masts. The woodcutter told his grandson that by paying attention to the details of each tree, and with experience in recognizing these characteristics, someday he too might become the woodcutter of the forest.

A little way into the forest, the grandson saw an old oak tree that had never been cut. The boy asked his grandfather if he could cut it down because it was useless for boat building - there were no straight limbs, the trunk was short and gnarled, and the curves were going the wrong way. "We could cut it down for firewood," the grandson said. "At least then it will be of some use to us." The woodcutter replied that for now they should be about their work cutting the proper trees for the boat builders; maybe later they could return to the old oak tree.

After a few hours of cutting the huge trees, the grandson grew tired and asked if they could stop for a rest in some cool shade. The woodcutter took his grandson over to the old oak tree, where they rested against its trunk in the cool shade beneath its twisted limbs. After they had rested a while, the woodcutter explained to his grandson the necessity of attentive awareness and recognition of everything in the forest and in the world.

Some things are readily apparent, like the tall, straight trees; other things are less apparent, requiring closer attention, like recognition of the proper curves in the limbs. And some things might initially appear to have no purpose at all, like the gnarled old oak tree. The woodcutter stated, "*You must learn to pay careful attention every day so you can recognize and discover the purpose God has for everything in creation. For it is this old oak tree, which you so quickly deemed useless except for firewood, that now allows us to rest against its trunk amidst the coolness of its shade. Remember, grandson, not everything is as it first appears. Be patient, pay attention, recognize, and discover.*"[6]

It is very unfortunate that many of us feel the same way. Our experiences with life's hardest blows and rejection has many many conclude that there is nothing worth living for because we don't see anything new springing forth. Like a dying tree losing leaves, we anticipate hopelessness daily, looking forward to more dreading days ahead. We roam the earth daily with no zest for purposeful living.

Like the oak tree, we think ignorance of purpose cancels it's value. However, just as the old oak tree had a distinct purpose of providing a shade for them after their hard day's work, you also have a distinct purpose ordained by God for you to do for humanity.

Just because you are ignorant of your worth does not mean you are not valuable. The old oak tree did not have a beautiful description; it was not recognized amongst the finest of the trees and even the grandson labeled it useless yet it's role was very significant. Your experiences in life may be looking ugly like the old oak tree- short and gnarled trunk, crooked limbs, and the curves going the wrong way but your life is a gift to the world.

Society may have despised you and ready to "cut you down" nevertheless you are here because God needs you here. The old oak tree was worthy so are you! It did not have beautiful stems but it was needed because it provided shade and a refuge for the grandfather and his grandson.

Stop despising your difference. Do you know that in spite of your insecurities and deficiencies, the world needs what you have?

Actually you are a masterpiece. The Greatest Mind designed you. He loves you and was very intentional when He created you.

Consider the scripture below:

> "For You formed my inward parts;
> You covered me in my mother's womb.
> I will praise you for I am fearfully and wonderfully made;
> Marvelous are Your works,
> And that my soul knows very well.
> My frame was not hidden from You,
> When I was made in secret,
> And skillfully wrought in the lowest parts of the earth.
> Your eyes saw my substance, being yet unformed.
> AND IN YOUR BOOK THEY WERE ALL WRITTEN,
> The days fashioned for me,
> When as yet there were none of them.
> You knew my innermost part.... all my members were written in your book."
>
> (PS. 139:13–16 NKJV, EMPHASIS ADDED)

The author of this text is David, and he was marveling at the awesomeness, careful thoughts and planning that God put into forming his human body; He took His time to carefully design his form and structure.

To be fearfully and wonderfully made can be best understood from an artistic or sculptural perspective. When an artist is designing or drawing a painting or sculpting an image, they take their time, exercising extreme care, so fearful to not mess up their finished products. He wanted you to be so unique and special that he made only you

Not only that, we also discovered that "all his members were written in His book" Hold on!

God has a book in heaven that has records of all our body parts? Isn't that amazing? Jesus further emphasized this truth when he said that the very hairs on our heads are numbered (Luke 12:7).

Now, even if you are not an English student you will agree with me that something that has been numbered would imply that not only has it been counted but there is a specific number allotted to it.

Hence, your hair strands, including all those that have fallen off, have numbers. If your hair has been numbered, how about your fingers, nose, legs and all the organs you don't even see? If He could carefully design your body, the house that shelters your spirit and soul, how much more could He design your purpose on earth?

This is the reason Jesus confidently said that he came in the volume of the book that was written concerning him (read Matthew 1:17), and it is also the very reason we shouldn't just be surviving but thrive in life by finding out God's original intention for creating us and pursue it confidently.

We Serve a Meticulous God Who Is Personally Interested in You!

God revealed His interest in our lives through many biblical characters. One of them was Jeremiah. God visited him one day, calling him into the office of a prophet when, being a son of a priest, he had decided to follow his father's footsteps to become a priest according to their Jewish custom. Scripture makes it clear that God interrupted his career choice and path when He introduced Himself as His Creator who knew him before he became a baby in his mother's womb and commissioned him for his prophetic mandate:

> "Before I formed you in the womb I knew you; Before you were born I sanctified you; I ordained you a prophet to the nations"
>
> (JER. 1:5).

There Is a Foreknowledge of You in God's Book in Heaven

Jeremiah's life further proved what David and Jesus were conveying, that none of our lives' details are accidental to God. As far as God was concerned, Jeremiah, then a seventeen-year-old teenager, was already a prophet ordained and sanctified even before he discovered he was so. Is it not interesting that in God's order of things, we are before we manifest?

In essence, God was telling Jeremiah that while he was about to follow tradition to accept the status quo or probably to impress his family, his career decision was going to end up being a life of failure because he would have missed God's purpose for his life. He may have been an awesome and faithful priest before the public but would have missed the mark. Imagine his life without God's intervention.

Everything was carefully crafted and planned and hence nothing surprises heaven about us. Can I free you today? That God is not shocked when you do certain things or make certain mistakes, and that He has already gone ahead of you and made the necessary provision for whatever situation and dreams He gives to you?

We Need to Reverse Engineer into the Blueprint of God for Our Lives

Just like Jeremiah, if God knew everything about you before you were born, then it also means that He knows beforehand what actions you will be taking in the next moment and also what He wanted you to do for Him on earth before the earth even existed. In other words, your purpose preceded your existence. Therefore, if He is calling you to an assignment, He has already put into your genetic and spiritual makeup the capacity to do it successfully.

This is what we call potential—your innate abilities that you have not yet used but are lying dormant in you. As far as God is concerned, you are already in your future now because He made you in eternity past. It's just a matter of time and a process of discovery and refinement for you to become that version. Therefore, reverse engineer into your glorious future which is already your finished end.

As God spoke to Jeremiah,

> "For I know the plans I think towards you, thoughts of peace and not of evil to give you an expected end"
>
> **(JER. 29:11).**

Your end in God is already expected. He is only waiting for you to get there.

MANDATE: Responding to Your Divine Commission

Just like Jeremiah, God has a book in heaven that chronicles everything about you: your body form, family tree, personality, and the mandate He has for you to fulfill. Now you may not have an angelic encounter like Mary or hear an audible voice like Jeremiah, but you must be certain that you are not an accident either, born to just roam on this planet, struggle, and die empty.

No, you were brought here on purpose, born within your race and in such a time as this to do some work for God, your Creator. This is what we call mandate.

While the dictionary defines the noun *mandate* as *"an official order or commission to do something; the authority given by people in leadership positions to carry out a policy or cause of action within their domain of influence"*[7], in the English grammar, the word mandate is a two part word: MAN and DATE.

In other words, you have a date with mankind. See it like having an appointment with someone with a given date and time which you are supposed to meet to fulfill the purpose of that appointment. That is exactly what our life is. We were brought on earth for an appointment with humanity with a certain time allotted and once our time is done, we will exit from this earth.

The mandate of God for you is to manifest itself in the various assignments He gives us from our position and roles at home, with our family to our workplace and the world at large. Every assignment given by God is essential and finishing them well, no matter how small or insignificant they may seem, matters in eternity. Therefore, mandate can be said to be the bundle of all the assignments that you will do on earth from the day you were born to the day you take your last breath for God.

Therefore, God in His book about Mary knew she was going to be the mother of His child and He knew everything about her spirit, soul, and body including that her womb was divinely chosen and prepared to carry and form the body of the Son of God and raise Him as an earthly son. Hence the greeting from Gabriel, the angel:

> "And having come in, the angel said to her, 'Rejoice, highly favored one, the Lord is with you; [a]blessed are you among women!'"
>
> (LUKE 1: 28 NKJV).

You Are Favored to Birth the Dreams & Visions of God

Mary was already favored before she discovered she was. Her womb was already created and chosen to carry Jesus. She was blessed above all women not because of something she did but because of what God already ordained for her life. She was the chosen virgin, prophesied by the Old Testament prophets to be the mother of the savior who would save the world of sin. God knew her in eternity past and I am here to remind you also that God knows you!

Regardless of your background or present circumstances, you have already been chosen by God to birth those visions and dreams He implanted in your spirit. This is the reason why those desires don't go down as much as many of us have tried to suppress or abort them altogether. He knew you would struggle with those ideas, yet He saw you qualified for the job. Therefore, brace yourself because you have also had the favor of God. If He chose you for it, then he also knows that you are equipped for the task ahead, while you may not feel prepared or qualified enough, trust that He's got you covered.

Whatever name God is calling you today, embrace it because in it lies the power to help you become it.

> "But as many as received Him, to them He gave the [a]right to become children of God, to those who believe in His name"
>
> (JOHN 1:12 NKJV).

The power in your becoming is hidden in your willingness to embrace Him and the task He is calling you to do for Him. So, repeat this after me: "I am valuable! I am wanted! I am forever loved! I am somebody because God does not create junk!

KEY TAKEAWAY : Your uniqueness is your power but, more importantly, what you do with it counts. Brace yourself for the challenge to develop yourself and your gifts because that is what will make you successful in your God-given assignment. Do You!

3

You Are God's Wildest Dream

A man was exploring caves by the seashore. In one of the caves he found a canvas bag with a bunch of hardened clay balls. It was like someone had rolled the clay balls and left them out in the sun to bake. They didn't look like much, but they intrigued the man, so he took the bag out of the cave with him.

As he strolled along the beach, he would throw the balls one at a time out into the ocean as far as he could. He thought little about it, until he dropped and it cracked open on a rock. Inside was a beautiful, precious stone - treasure in clay!

Excited, the man started breaking open the remaining clay balls. Each contained a similar treasure. He found thousands of dollars worth of jewels in the 20 or so balls he had left.

Then it struck him. He had been on the beach a long time. He had thrown maybe 50 or 60 of the balls with their hidden treasure in the clay into the ocean waves. Instead of thousands of dollars in treasure, he could have taken home tens of thousands, but he had just thrown it away.[8] Sad truth huh?

I have the same question for you: are you busy looking for significance and value outside of yourself? If you are, then let me reassure you that what you are searching outside resides inside of you. Also, let's be mindful and stop looking down on others because of their external limitations and flaws as they do not diminish their value in God.

2 Corinthians 4:7 makes it clear to us that we indeed possess treasure:

> "But we have this treasure in earthen vessels, that the excellence of the power may be of God and not of us."

We are the vessels of clay. In Genesis 2:7, the bible also narrates that

> "God formed man of the dust of the ground, and breathed into his nostrils the breath of life; and man became a living being."

These two scriptures make it clear that although our bodies are made of clay, we are beyond our bodies. In fact, this body is housing a treasure and if we take the time to get to discover our true selves through the lens of our Creator by allowing the Holy Spirit to reveal our genius to us, then the clay that has been blinding us will begin to peel away for the gem in us to radiate to serve God's purposes and to glorify Him.

In the previous chapter, we learned that nothing about our life is accidental; your existence on this planet right now proves someone somewhere needs you. So, how do you express the purpose God wired you to perform? Well, the answer is simple: through the visions and dreams He deposited in you (treasure) and through the way He wired you to express through the various circumstances and situations that unfold during your lifetime (the excellence of God's power)

Understanding Dreams and Visions

> "And it shall come to pass afterward That I will pour out My Spirit on all flesh; Your sons and your daughters shall prophesy, Your old men shall dream dreams, Your young men shall see visions"
>
> **(JOEL 2:28 NKJV).**

Did you know that your dreams and visions are not just about you? God gave them to you, and, when you play your part, He adds to His overall corporate purpose and plan for humanity?

The above scripture is a clear indicator of the generational impact of our dreams and visions. God was speaking through His prophet, Joel on what an outpouring of His Spirit looks like. This is the picture of true revival: sons and daughters prophesying, old men dreaming dreams, and young men seeing visions.

Therefore, realizing your dreams and visions is not always about you. Establishing generational inheritance should give us the urgency to pursue the whispers of purpose from our hearts because it has never been about us. Some of you have been given the responsibility to break certain generational curses and establish new generational foundations that your children and grandchildren will reap the reward of your labor.

ANATOMY OF DREAMS AND VISIONS

Dreams are living mental pictures or experiences that occur while sleeping. However, a vision happens while you are awake. Therefore, a dream occurs while you are unconscious while a vision happens when you are fully aware of your surroundings yet in a different state of consciousness.

Biologically, older adults don't have the strength and stamina of their youth so they dream. They usually tend to reflect about their past glory and of what is to come.

On the other hand, a younger person has the strength and youthful vigor to achieve their goals and, because they are mostly in their prime, they tend to get a lot done faster physically and mentally. They see visions because naturally, a young person has sharper eye sight and can see more clearly than an older person's dim eyes. Vision also involves the following factors: careful planning, clarity, goals, and objectives; actually, it takes a young man's vision to see an old man's dream.

This is the reason why Habakkuk 2:2 tells us to write down the vision and make it plain so he who reads it can run with it. The young person in this context, reads the vision(s), and "runs" with it. They have the strength to run unlike their older counterparts. Hence, a dream is geared towards the future while a vision is a dream realized in the present. Therefore, walking in your dreams turns the dream into a vision.

Ideally, the older generation who no longer possess physical vigor but are rich in wisdom and experience, nonetheless can help the younger generation by offering counsel, wisdom, and directions as they run with the baton that has been passed down to them. This is what is known as trans-generational impact.

The Power of Legacy

> "Legacy is the leg you see. It's not legacy until the next generation is able to walk out what it is that you built."
> — STEPHEN CHESTNUT[9]

The Bible has various examples of the relationship between a dreamer and visionary. However, it is imperative we understand that whether you have a dream or you are currently walking out a vision, the effects are the same. The only difference is the timing and implementation.

Perhaps the best biblical example of how God intended the dynamics of dreams and visions can be found in the life of Jesus. He came on earth by the Father's wishes, because the Father had a dream of restoring his broken relationship with humanity. And He knew the only way divine justice would be served would be when the blood of an innocent person is shed (Heb. 9:22). Therefore, the Father went into some negotiation with His Son who willfully offered Himself to be the sacrificial lamb so the Father's desires can be fulfilled.

However, for this plan to work, God had to cooperate with a human being. This is how God then gave a young woman a vision of bearing His son in her womb without her husband's involvement. As you can see, while Mary was carrying out a vision from God, she was technically realizing the Dream in God's heart by following His plan to making it happen.

Jesus further realized His Father's plan by recruiting twelve disciples. He believed in them and trained them to carry the baton of reaching the whole world with the help of the Holy Spirit. You see,

Jesus's vision to train disciples was locked in the dream of His Heavenly Father of having the whole world reconciled to Him.

Thus, as He went about working on the vision set before Him, which was dying on the cross, Jesus was already "dreaming" about the next chapter, which was going to be carried by His successors, the disciples who would then be empowered by the Holy Spirit to take the gospel to the whole world, and guess what: Jesus was only thirty-three years old when He accomplished His mission on earth.

This makes me understand that you don't have to be seventy years old to start dreaming and starting a succession plan. The moment you start implementing a vision you should also be intentionally dreaming for the next generation, that is if you have already started. The dream is free! You don't have to have a special ability before you can dream. Use your imagination and paint some awesome canvas about your future and the future of the next generation.

In our modern time, we see that the late renowned civil rights leader and activist, Dr. Martin Luther King Junior once gave a speech in which he said he had a dream. He went further to say that one day, His children would be judged by the content of their character; not by the color of their skin. This was more than six decades ago.

Well, while Dr. King may not be alive today, it is clear that the world we currently live in is closer to his dream than it was in his generation. You see, when the United States first elected an African American man into the highest office in the land, the then President-elect gave a speech in which he acknowledged himself being an actualization of Dr. Martin Luther King's dream:

> "This election had many firsts and many stories that will be told for generations. But one that's on my mind tonight's about a woman who cast her ballot in Atlanta. She's a lot like the millions of others who stood in line to make their voice heard in this elec-

tion except for one thing: Ann Nixon Cooper is 106 years old. She was born just a generation past slavery, a time when there were no cars on the road or planes in the sky, when someone like her couldn't vote for two reasons—because she was a woman and because of the color of her skin... At a time when women's voices were silenced and their hopes dismissed, she lived to see them stand up and speak out and reach for the ballot...She was there for the buses in Montgomery, the hoses in Birmingham, a bridge in Selma, and a preacher from Atlanta who told a people that 'We Shall Overcome'."[10]

President Obama represented Dr. Martin Luther King's children's generation, and to have him elected as president in a nation that once regarded African Americans as second-class citizens was way beyond the dream of that generation. President Obama's election proved that Dr. King's dream of having his children judged by the content of their character was now being realized through the vision of the next generation. While Dr. King didn't live to see it, his children and the generation after were all living in that reality. We are walking out what their generation built. That is the power of a dream. This is what happens when you dream, it means you are passing the "baton" to the next person who will carry on with the assignment you started. Therefore, you don't have to grow old or wear out to start dreaming.

While you are working on a vision, start dreaming for the next generation and begin writing a succession plan for your successor to run with it and dream further. This is how we continue the chain of legacy. Remember they need to "see" and "walk out" what you have built.

The Power of Imagination

"I pray that the light of God will illuminate the eyes of your imagination, flooding you with light, until you experience the full revelation of the hope of his calling—that is, the wealth of God's glorious inheritances that he finds in us, his holy ones!"

(EPH. 1:18 THE PASSION TRANSLATION).

The gift of imagination is the gateway to our creativity and potential. The above scripture was part of the Apostle Paul's introduction to his epistle to the Ephesian Church. As the founding father of the church he heard about the works of the flesh that were being exhibited among the members and he was about to lay the groundwork for the doctrine of the church today. Paul was praying that the church would interpret his letters through the lens of enlightenment, which also is expressed through their imagination guided by the Holy Spirit.

Likewise, we can all imagine endless possibilities. Actually, all of us have the gift of imagination and we do it naturally. This means that even a blind person can imagine. They may be visually impaired, but they are not blinded in their vision inwardly. This is because imagination is an invisible spiritual organ that resides between our spirit, soul, and body. It is described in the Greek as *phantasia*, which means "*a live show, performance, or motion picture*"[1] -like a movie.

Just as a presenter uses a projector to screen their thoughts, likewise our imagination is the screen that our visions and dreams are projected on. Imagination is a lens through which visions and dreams are expressed inwardly. Because imagination is neutral, what we envision determines the outcome, and because it is at the center of the spirit, soul, and body, you can project images from God, the devil, or yourself. Imagination gives us the ability to not only receive the mental images or movies, but we also can choose to use this wonderful gift from God to envision our outcome. This means you can imagine wrong thoughts and you can also imagine awesome things. You can choose to create an awesome future and life with the power of your imagination.

In fact, science has proven that what you imagine in your mind and your actual reality are no different as your body experiences them as the same. This is the reason why the Bible commissions us to be mindful about what goes in our thoughts because we birth what we imagine,

> "as a man thinketh in his heart, so is he"
> **(PROV. 23:7).**

Every man-made invention you see existing in our world today started as thoughts and mental "movies" in someone's mind in what we call ideas. Anytime you picture something, your imagination is connected to it. The chair in which we sit, to the laptops and cell phones we use, even this book all started as ideas. And the more they were focused and meditated on, the more their inventors got details on how to birth them, thus the ideas became manifested. Hence, thoughts are very powerful because they become things.

What you think matters. In the spirit realm, there is no difference between what you think and your physical reality. This is the reason Jesus once said that if a man lusts after a woman, he has already slept with her in her heart. Why? Because a man can't lust after a woman without imagining doing lustful things with her. Because your imagination is premeditated, it becomes your desires and you end up birthing it. There is no difference in it actualizing as far as

God is concerned, because you have conceived it in your heart, you have already birthed it.

Now you see how powerful imagination is? This is also the reason why God admonishes us to:

> "cast down every imaginations and every high thing that exalts the knowledge of God, bringing every thought into captivity to the obedience of Christ"
>
> (2 COR. 10:5).

Because those things come from either our flesh or from the devil, and if we give our lens of imagination to them, they will manifest in the natural world.

The best gift you can give to yourself therefore, is to get tuned in with God; read His Word (the Bible) and meditate on His promises concerning you. Then begin to listen with your spirit and allow Him to paint "movies" through the lens of your imagination. You will be amazed by the great things you will accomplish through that. Suddenly ideas, solutions, and innovations will be coming out through your lens of imagination, and because you are feeding yourself with the living Word of God you will start enjoying a good successful life.

Most of all the inward dreams and visions that come to us are not really premeditated; they are usually projections from God through our spirits. More often than not, they are things that are stirred by our purpose, but they are already in you. You'd be surprised that God has been speaking to you all the time through imagination and if only you will pay attention to your inward dreams and visions, you'd be amazed at the outcome you will produce. Just think for a moment how Mark Zuckerberg thought he was inventing a social network in order to socialize with girls only for it to become a social networking giant called Facebook, which has united the whole world and is serving a universal purpose. That was only one idea, which was expressed through the lens of imagination.

You too can use your imagination to get yourself out of any situation you find yourself in today. Now imagine yourself as the president of your country. How about the first female trailblazer in your family to go to college and become a CEO of the best company of your niche or the bestselling author, speaker, coach, etc. How would it feel like to be the one to break those generational dysfunctional patterns in your family by being the first of everything? If you can imagine it, you can birth it!

Use your imagination to break through those ceilings over your head, further your dreams and watch them manifesting right before your eyes as you pursue your visions. Imagination will give you the confidence to take the first leap of faith.

KEY TAKEAWAY: You are God's wildest dream. What you consider dreams or visions are actually an extension of God's dream for humanity. Therefore, be confident and, as you step out to implement your dreams, never stop dreaming and planning for trans-generational impact.

4

Dream and Vision Expressions

While the dreams and visions from God serve the same purpose, their expressions in our lives are never the same. This is because we serve a dynamic God who loves to show His creativity in the ways He deals with all His children. In this chapter we are going to find out the various ways God expresses dreams and visions in our lives.

Ways God Express His Dreams and Visions in Our Lives

You must realize that while not everyone is going to see an angel showing them their divine assignment(s), God still has work for you. Listed below are some of the ways that God reveals His assignment(s) in our lives. I've categorized them below based on different ways God revealed His plans for the characters in the Bible. Maybe yours could fit in one of them.

1. THE WORD OF FAITH

> For what does the Scripture say? "Abraham believed God, and it was accounted to him for righteousness."
>
> ROM. 4:3 NKJV)

Abraham in the Bible is known to be the father of many nations and the Patriarch of faith. In fact, in chapter 11 of the book of Hebrews, in what theologians term as the hallmark of faith, it is written specifically why God credited to him righteousness:

> "By faith Abraham obeyed when he was called to go out to the place which he would receive as an inheritance. And he went out, not knowing where he was going. By faith he dwelt in the land of promise as *in* a foreign country, dwelling in tents with Isaac and Jacob, the heirs with him of the same promise; for he waited for the city which has foundations, whose builder and maker *is* God"
>
> HEB. 11:8-10 (NKJV)

You must realize that Abraham became a man of faith not because he saw visions but because He heard a word from God to move from his native land into the land He would show him (Gen. 12:1). Abraham's daringness to follow the instruction from God without a clear cut direction is a sign of radical faith walking—taking God literally at His word.

Today, God still speaks to certain people through that means; not dreaming, visions, or angelic encounters but just one word from God. Sometimes, people experience this through the reading of the *Logos*[10] (Greek for the written word of God, also known as the Bible).

When the Holy Spirit breathes upon His Word and the Spirit of revelation takes over, the written word of God can become a prophetic word to you. This is what is known in the Greek as *Rhema*[11] in an individual's life. While every word written in the bible is inspired (God breathed), according to 2 Timothy 3:16, when the Holy Spirit highlights or brings to our attention, a particular verse or portion of scripture that become application to our personal and unique situation, that becomes God's Prophetic word to you.

At other times, a person may experience a nudge or a prompting in their spirit without having any tangible proof or evidence yet they know within that it is the voice of God speaking to them. While they can't prove it with tangible things, they are convinced in their spirits that they've heard God's voice and they proceed to go into an adventure with Him. Therefore, if you find yourself on this side of the coin—with just one word of instruction from God—and you have still not taken a step because you didn't see a vision, dream, or have an angelic encounter, you are missing your moments with God.

Abraham is a prime example that God can give you one word or instruction and not be specific yet He still expects you to take a step in the voice of instruction, trusting Him to be with you in the process.

2. THE DREAMERS & VISIONARIES

In Genesis, a young man was introduced to us who had been having vivid prophetic dreams about his destiny at the age of seventeen. His name was Joseph. In Genesis 37, Scripture relates that Joseph had two dreams that meant the same thing: he was going to be great and they would pay homage to him.

This got his brothers to hate him the more and they even intended to kill him until they finally decided to sell him into slavery. However, God through the turn of events and life processes manifested those dreams fourteen years later. You might see yourself in this type of person. You are very visionary and dreamy. You tend to see your dreams actualize. Well, you are a Joseph! God reveals His purposes for you through dreams and visions. He gives you specific details about your future. If you find yourself in this category, congratulations.

This book will show you how to overcome the frustrations of waiting, honing your skills as you cultivate your gifts and learning how to exercise self-control in the passage of time to protect the visions God has given you.

3. DIVINE ENCOUNTERS

These are people who received their divine assignments through supernatural encounters, such as Jesus, angels, or heavenly beings appearing to them. Examples in the Bible are Saul on the road to Damascus and later encountering Jesus, which changed his life forever. Mary, the mother of Jesus also had an angelic encounter which would presage the birth Jesus. Zachariah, the priest who would become the father of John the Baptist, Samson's Parents, Abraham, entertained their angelic visitors Lot welcoming the two angels and many others. People in this category tend to receive specific instructions from angels concerning the promises of God for them or what they ought to do to be effective in their mandates.

4. PERSONALITIES, PASSION & SENSES

There are three men in the Bible who encountered God through their personalities, senses, a or emotions and as a result became spiritual giants who were mightily used by God to affect their generation: Moses, Paul, and Samson.

Forty years down the road in his escape, Moses would encounter God through his sense of curiosity:

> And the Angel of the Lord appeared to him in a flame of fire from the midst of a bush. So he looked, and behold, the bush was burning with fire, but the bush was not consumed. Then Moses said, "*I will now turn aside to see this great sight, why the bush does not burn*" so when the Lord saw that he turned aside to look, God called to him from the midst of the bush and said, "*Moses, Moses!*" And he said, "*Here I am*"
>
> (EX. 3:2-4)

The rest, they say, is history. Clearly God used Moses's senses to direct his path and used them to get him to respond to His dream for Moses's life, which would make him a deliverer in the hands of God who would deliver His people from 400 years of oppression, in what would become known as the Exodus.

Paul, then Saul, on the other hand, was a Pharisee who persecuted the first century church because he felt they were teaching erroneous doctrines. Paul saw it fit to persecute the "vagabonds" who posed a threat to the Mosaic Torah so he could preserve the legacy. However, he would soon discover through his encounter with Jesus on the road to Damascus that clearly, his cause to persecute the church was actually a passion that has been displaced.

After his conversion, Paul became the Apostle to the Gentiles, and God clearly used the same drive Paul had to defend the gospel, to write two thirds of the New Testament and to champion the cause of the gospel, planting churches, raising leaders, and pioneering new moves for the Glory of God.

Samson, the strongest man, recording in the Bible and the Book of Judges to the people of Israel also was used by God countless times through his temperament to kill the enemies of Israel. First, he used an unsolved riddle to kill thirty Philistines (Judg 14:1-20). Then, he got angry and, feeling betrayed by his father-in-law, for not giving his wife to him, he went out and caught 300 foxes and tied their tails together in pairs, securing burning torches to their tails, and setting them free to run for their lives in the Philistine's fields. This got more Philistines killed.

Then, after the Philistines discovered Samson was the culprit behind their burnt fields, they also burned his father-in-law and wife. This got him even more angry, and he set out to do more damage and killed more of them as revenge (Judg. 15).

As you can see, Samson's anger got him to do more damage and killed more of his enemies. Needless to say, God sovereignly used his temperament to accomplish the purpose of raising him as a judge to conform to the purpose of His will for Israel.

God used the personalities and senses of these great men to usher them into the dreams and mandate He had for them. Likewise, God is still at work in our lives. The late Dr. Myles Munroe once said, *"where purpose is not known, abuse is inevitable."*[12] Most of the time, the things we despise about ourselves or in others could be clues that could lead you to His purpose for your life. It could be displaced passion, which can be turned into the powerful weapon in the hands of the Almighty God to fulfill His purpose.

5. DIVINE PROVIDENCE

This is when God works behind the scenes. No one's life fits beautifully in this example more than that of Esther in the Bible. She was captured, taken against her will to be a contestant or a potential new bride for the emperor of Persia. The book of Esther relates that the king's former wife, Vashti, rebelled against her husband and as a result brought shame to the throne. Due to counsel, the king was advised to choose a new bride from the province.

Hence, Esther (then Hadassah), became a victim of this situation. However, as it would turn out, God indeed would let her become the queen of the empire to fulfill His greater purpose later—saving His chosen people where were now in exile, as part of the people in the king's rulership—all "behind the scenes."

Perhaps what stands out for me in the book of Esther is the fact that God's name or His persona was never mentioned in it yet somehow He was still working everything out together for the corporate good of His people even when they felt God had neglected them and allowed them to be taken into exile. Through Esther's life we learn that what we usually consider to be coincidences are often divine providence in action. God has already anticipated the turn of events; He went ahead of you.

Many of us will bump into God's dream(s) for us through this route. You may not have all the supernatural means of revelation of purpose but just because He is not speaking directly to you like others does not mean He is not working for you. If you find yourself on this side of the coin, rest assured that you are still right in the center of God's will for your life. You may not understand your journey but trust the process.

6. WHEN PAIN PRODUCES PURPOSE

Have you ever felt your life is not wanted yet somehow good seems to find you out? Well that is the case of David, who would later be our beloved giant slayer, worshiper, king, and awesome song writer. The first time we were introduced to him was when a man was recommending his harp-playing skills to the demon tormented king (1 Sam. 16:16).

Later we discover that clearly God has appointed David to be the next in line for the throne of Israel which would require the prophet, Samuel, going into his father's house to anoint him before his family. Through his father's response when he presented his sons and left David out we discovered that David was actually neglected.

This was a clear indicator that something about David's family dynamic was off, and theologians actually believed that David was born into sin. He wasn't considered a legitimate son because he was a product of adultery. It is believed that this is what instigated Psalm 51:5 which he wrote, *"[I]n sin did my mother conceive me"*

Hence, it makes sense for his father to send his son, as vulnerable as he was, into the back side of the desert, with all the risks involved, but the beautiful picture here shows that his father's rejection allowed David to fall into the loving arms of our Heavenly Father and we would later see the fruit of the beautiful union they shared being demonstrated in all the exploits God would use him to do.

We discover that God was actually using these life-threatening situations to prepare David for the tasks ahead. A beautiful example was when Saul tried to give him his armor and David confidently said to him that God had trained him for war, the unconventional way, through the killing of a lion and bear, so he was confident he could defeat Goliath.

Another biblical example is Naomi and Ruth. After losing everything and going back with her mother-in-law to her native land,

Ruth was given another chance to be part of the genealogy of Jesus by marrying Boaz, who became the father of Obed, the grandfather of David, from whom Joseph, the earthly father of Jesus, was going to come.

What do you do when life's situation chooses you—when you find your assignment or purpose through the pain of the trauma you experience in your life? When through the turn of events that have happened to you, you suddenly find your "why" and then everything begins to make sense why you want to champion a cause.

I am sure all of us have witnessed people like this who have encountered different situations and challenges that tried to cripple them yet by God's grace these people have found their wings to fly through their own brokenness to make someone's life better than what they've endured. Have you been a victim of violence, rape, injustice, or some unpleasant situation or other disabilities? Have you found a way to weather that storm? Could it be that maybe God, in His love, while He didn't do those negative things to you may be using the scenario as a vehicle or a launching pad to your purpose.

7. LEGACY CARRIERS

These are the people I call successors. They are those who inherit dreams or visions from a predecessor, and then continue to run with the baton to continue the legacy.

There are people today who are not born to be pioneers. Nonetheless, their contribution in preserving legacies is equally important. Every vision presented to mortals is destined to be wiped away unless they are successful passed on to the right people to carry them on.

These are people whose gifts are discovered early, and sometimes their life destiny is prophesied so they are groomed from the get go to carry the baton forward. Examples of biblical characters of this include Solomon and Joshua.

Solomon was the golden son of King David. Technically the second son of Bathsheba, he was the promised child who was the heir to the throne of his father, David, and the vessel chosen by God to build the temple that his father had wanted to build for God. Solomon was fortunate to get some training from his dad as his successor and he successfully transferred his throne to David.

Joshua was also the successor of Moses. He was successful in carrying out the mandate that was rightly laid out by Moses, his mentor. He didn't deliver the Israelites from Egypt, but he was part of the delivered and also stayed with Moses through the forty-year wandering in the wilderness. Because of his close proximity, he saw everything first hand and got many opportunities to serve his mentor. God also described him as having a different spirit (Numbers 14:24).

Therefore, Joshua was a very effective successor who helped the generation born in the wilderness to inherit the promise land.

You may find yourself on this side of the world. You find yourself being positioned either by choice or sovereignly being placed by God to serve in the vision of a pioneer or an institution. Sometimes you have a strong drive and desire or other creative ideas and ways to improve things for the leadership or the overall betterment of the place where you find yourself.

Even if you are not exactly sure if you are going to inherit anything, I'd urge you to pour yourself completely into the vision of the institution and serve with everything you have. We need preservers of legacy to sustain the immortality of a vision.

KEY TAKEAWAY: We serve a dynamic God who doesn't do the

same thing twice when it comes to our dream and vision expressions, so embrace your unique journey, carved by God for you.

5

What the Heck Am I Doing?

Mary was very smart with her interaction with the angel. After Gabriel had finished speaking, she didn't just get up to say that's it, let's go! We are getting pregnant and pushing this God out! Rather she asked one question that got us to see how God was about to unfold His plan for her:

> "Then Mary said to the angel, 'How can this be, I am a Virgin?'"
>
> **(LUKE 1: 34 NKJV)**.

The Power of Asking

Years ago, there lived a wise and noble king. The king lived a happy life with his beautiful wife. Then, only a few years after their marriage, his wife got very sick. Sadly, she died soon after. Unfortunately, this tragedy occurred before having children, leaving the king to rule the kingdom alone, without his bride beside him. While devastated by the loss of his wife, the king stayed true to his commitment to rule with honor and take care of the people in his kingdom.

The love for his wife was so strong, the king couldn't bear the thought of ever getting married again. So as the years passed, having no children of his own, the king knew the time would come where he would have to find the right man who, upon his death, would take his place as king. Since there was no bloodline and no son who could rightfully take the king's place, he called upon the people of the kingdom to help him find a suitable heir to the throne.

The king knew there would have to be a test of some sort that would help identify the most promising candidate. One day, while the king was taking a stroll through the countryside, he came upon a massive sinkhole. It was so large that you could fit at least two soccer fields inside of it. *"I've got it!"* exclaimed the King. *"I know the test that would help me identify the next king."* And with that, he quickly returned to the castle to share his idea with his advisors.

The very next day, the king issued a decree throughout the kingdom. *"Come one, come all. In three weeks' time, those who feel worthy enough to take my place will meet in the town square to demonstrate why you are the one who should be the heir to the kingdom."* The day finally arrived. It seemed as if thousands of people traveled for miles to reach the town square; from every corner of the kingdom, with the dream of being chosen as the heir to the throne.

The king took these promising candidates out to the countryside to show them what he had found. *"Here is the question that, if answered correctly, will earn you the rightful place as our next king."* Pointing to the massive hole, he simply asked, *"What should I do?"*

After several days and hundreds of responses later, no one had yet to come up with the right answer. Repeatedly, the king would hear the same responses. *"Fill it with rocks and dirt." "Fill it with water." "Build a bridge across the sinkhole." "Build a wall around it." "Put warning signs around the sinkhole." "Make it a graveyard." "Leave it be." "Camouflage the sinkhole to protect us from our enemies."* While some of these may be interesting ideas, none of them were the correct answer.

The king was getting discouraged, wondering if anyone was capable of thinking and acting like a successful king. As the number of candidates dwindled to a remaining few, it was time for one young man to answer the king's question; a poor farm boy from the countryside who was ridiculed by those older and wiser than he for even considering the possibility of becoming king. "So," the king began with a disheartened and skeptical tone. *"What should I do?"*

The young man hesitated for a moment and then responded with, *"Why do anything?"*

Suddenly, the king's disposition changed. He looked at the young man and asked with hope, *"Why? When everyone else advised me what I could do with the sinkhole, why are you the only one not to advise me at all, nor tell me what I should do? Why do you come to me with only a question?"* The young man respectfully answered. *"Because I cannot answer your question, my king. I don't know your why. Until I understand not just what you want to do but why you want to do anything about this sinkhole and your intentions behind it, only then can I advise you to create your desired outcome, even if the proper course of action is to do nothing."*

Instead of telling the king what he would do, this young man simply asked the king one question. A question so simple, yet so powerful and often overlooked. *"Why?"* After all, how can you align and collaborate effectively with others if you don't understand their motivations, intention and their why behind their beliefs, efforts, actions, opinions, decisions, behavior, goals or values?

"Congratulations," exclaimed the king. *"You are the next heir to the throne of our kingdom."* The town was shocked. The elders of the town questioned the king. *"Why this boy?"*

To which the king replied, *"I never wanted to fix anything. That was not my intention. Everyone came to me with a solution to fixing what they assumed was a problem that needed fixing. They never took the time to uncover and understand my why or my desired intentions and point of view. This young man was the only one who was insightful enough to seek out my intention and uncover my why."*[5]

A lot of us make mistakes with the execution of God's vision. Many of us fail to consult God first before implementing the ideas, dreams and visions He gives us. We do not make time to seek Him for strategies and wisdom on to proceed. Rather, we assume our own way and we wonder why we become unsuccessful and many of us end up aborting great visions and dreams that could have impacted the world for Jesus.

However, time and time again, Jesus literally commands us to be daring in asking because we will receive answers:

> *"Ask it will be given unto you"*
>
> **(MATT. 7:7 NKJV).**

> *"And whatever you ask in My name, that I will do, that the Father may be glorified in the Son. If you [a]sk anything in My name, I will do it"*
>
> **(JOHN 14:13–14).**

A lot of us make a big mistake when it comes to the execution of God's vision. What the majority of us fail to do right away when we get an idea from God is not asking what the strategies of how it will be done might be, rather we assume our own way and we wonder why we become unsuccessful and many of us end up aborting great visions and dreams that could have impacted the world for Jesus.

Mary asking the angel how it was going to be done was the right step to uncovering God's strategy for implementing His plan of manifesting His Son on earth.

If we don't ask the right questions, how are we going to get the right answers?

You must realize that although your vision is legitimately from God, the implementation of it is tailored to your unique calling, gifts, and skill set. Sometimes, how God will manifest it will be completely different from how everyone else manifests their dreams. This is the reason the Bible is very clear that it is unwise to compare yourself with everyone else (2 Cor. 10:12).

By asking the question of how it was going to be done, Mary was setting herself up to get the answers of how God was going to implement His plan through her.

Should she have assumed that just because she is engaged, it would mean that maybe after she had finally settled down with Joseph as her husband then they will have the Savior; she would have missed God!

Yes, Mary had heard the angel all right, but it was up to her to ask the right questions to get the right answers to making his message a reality.

What questions are you asking God today concerning that idea He gave you? Yes, I know it will impact the world, but are you seeking God's help to understand exactly how to execute them or do you think you are smarter than God Himself?

The beautiful thing about asking questions is there is always an answer; God promises to answer us when we call. Jesus commands us to bombard Heaven with our questions, so why are we not asking? After all, He provides Himself as the answer.

Asking Questions Exposes Your Vulnerability and Creates Dependability on God

"Trust in the Lord with all your heart and lean not on your own understanding. In all your ways, acknowledge Him and He will direct your paths"

(PROV. 3:5).

When you ask the right questions, it shows that you don't know what you are doing and that is okay! When Mary asked the angel the question, it was obvious that she was acknowledging that, although she had a fiancé, she still didn't want to assume that her son was going to come from Joseph because Joseph's name was never mentioned.

I am reminded of the story of Moses when he was killing himself to serve the people of Israel. He thought sweating and struggling was the way to go until Jethro, his father-in-law showed up and told him, "Like hey, dude, what you are lacking is administration and management. You are not a Superman so stop trying to do it by yourself and micromanage everything. Instead delegate a leader from each tribe and assign them a task so they report to you" (read the entire narrative in Exodus chapter 18).

That was a counsel from God but it came through his father-in-law. All Moses had to do was ask God, "please how do I govern your people?" Instead, he thought he knew best and God too was silent, watching how far things would go. This is what sometimes happens to some of us—instead of asking God for directions on what He gives us, we tend to think we know what we are doing and exhaust all our resources; then we become burnt out, blaming God when we are not succeeding.

But let me make this statement clear for you: If you are trying to micromanage the vision God gave you, quit now!

God didn't call you to do anything independent of Him; He didn't call you to rise up and do it all on your own. You have His help! But in order to tap into that help, you must be willing to admit that you don't know what you are doing so you can align yourself to receive His resources, and the first step in this direction is asking questions: how can this be?

Don't be afraid to ask questions about the visions God gives you. There can never be a wrong or stupid question; the more questions you ask, the more answers you get and the more clarity He gives you.

It's Okay When You Don't Know What You Are Doing!

"Your Assignment from God will make you a Virgin"[16]

—DR MYLES MONROE.

Back to Mary's question to the angel, we will soon discover that the reason why she asked that question was because she was a virgin. And accordingly, she knew it was impossible to have a baby without a male involvement. To have a baby in the natural way, you must have sexual intercourse with a man for him to release a sperm that fertilizes an egg for the cycle of pregnancy to begin, and in Mary's situation, she was still not yet married when the angel approached her with the baby announcement so the obvious logical question would be how that was going to happen.

After all, if she was already married and, in her little human mind, the question would have been irrelevant, but in this case, it was not possible and she was a virgin; she had never had sex with a man before.

Theologically speaking and in relation to our subject, the term *virgin* is defined as someone who has never had sex before or simply put, was completely inexperienced sexually.[17] Whatever God is asking you to do, you are going to be inexperienced; you will be put in a situation where your confidence will be questioned because you will be naive and innocent about it—a virgin!

Surprisingly, and contrary to popular opinion, your ignorance in the scope of God's assignment for you is an asset because it allows you to rely completely on God every step of the way, which also gives Him the room to do what only He can do: empower you to do the impossible. By being liable in the natural, you become unstoppable in the spiritual because you tap into the grace of God, which catapults you into the realm of possibilities.

God will make us uncomfortable and take us from a place we don't feel qualified for the task He has given us so we can keep leaning on and trusting Him every step of the way. Now, let me make this disclaimer: it will feel scary at times and we may even feel intimidated by it. but that is where trust comes in. You've got to give Him your 100 percent!

Do you have a Dream from God that looks impossible or unnatural for it to happen? Well, my friend, give it to God! He didn't call you to depend on your skills, talents, intellect etc. He knew you didn't have what it takes, but He also knows that if you will partner with Him, He can accomplish that dream through you. So no, you can't do it by your own accord, but yes you can because you have Him and all things are possible with Him. For that to happen, there needs to be a divine exchange where you give Him your weakness so He can give you His strength. This exchange is what we call supernatural; He puts His *super* on your *natural* and together, you do fantastic exploits.

What is stopping you today from stepping out and taking the first step? Are you lacking confidence to write the first sentence of that book, sing the first line of the song, dial that number to request for that interview, promotion, proposal or start that business? Whatever the Lord is impressing on your heart to do, remember it is not going to be by your own strength. He is ready to help you.

God Has Various Ways He Speaks to Us Concerning the Visions and Dreams He Places on Our Heart.

God Guides Us Through His Written Word

God's written word has and will always be God's voice of authority to counsel, direct, rebuke, and show us how to live and be fulfilled in life.

Consider the following scriptures:

"For the word of God is living and powerful, and sharper than any two-edged sword, piercing even to the division of soul and spirit, and of joints and marrow, and is a discerner of the thoughts and intents of the heart" (Heb. 4:12 NKJV).

"You have magnified Your word above all Your name" (Ps. 138:2 NKJV).

"Your word is a lamp to my feet And a light to my path" (Ps. 119:105).

"I have chosen the way of truth; Your judgments I have laid before me" (Ps. 119:130 NKJV).

"I am the Lord your God, Who teaches you to profit, Who leads you by the way you should go"

(Isa. 48:17 NKJV).

These scriptures are letting us know God's word is our life's manual and if we will live our lives on it, we will be enlightened in our pursuit of our life mandate.

God Uses the Voices of People He Has Placed in Our Lives

HE USES VOICES OF AUTHORITY IN OUR LIVES

Back to Moses's story, we learned the Jethro, his father-in-law, after observing Moses's lack of organizational structure gave him sound advice that not only revolutionized his leadership but also saved his life. Moses listened to him; let's look at the role Jethro played in his life.

Exodus 2 relates that after Moses fled from Pharaoh after killing an Egyptian, he landed in Midian, where he was welcomed by Jethro, the priest, after helping his daughters draw water from the well. Jethro then goes on to not only take care of Moses by providing food, clothing, and shelter, he also offered his daughter, Zipporah, to him in marriage, and trained and ordained Moses into the Melchizedek priesthood. Moses, in turn, became a shepherd who watched over his father-in-law's flocks.

From all accounts Jethro was more than just a fatherly figure in Moses's life. He became a very influential voice of authority, who taught him the way of the Lord. Hence, he heeded the counsel that Jethro gave him concerning his leadership style.

Another biblical example is found in 1 Samuel, when the young boy, Samuel, heard the voice of God but thought it was the voice of his father, Eli, the priest. It was Eli who gave him counsel on what to do with the voice he heard and how he should respond.

Sometimes, our prayers are not answered directly from God because He has already positioned certain people who serve as His voice of authority in our lives and if only we will seek their counsel concerning the dreams that God places in our hearts, their advice can take us to the next level of progress that we were missing.

Who is God's voice of authority in your life? God didn't leave us stranded to fend for yourselves.

HE SPEAKS THROUGH THE EVERYDAY PEOPLE WE MEET ON A DAILY BASIS

God doesn't just speak through the people who have been placed in leadership positions over us. He speaks through the everyday people that many of us even sometimes take for granted. A typical example in the Bible is found in 2 Kings 5, when the slave girl living with her master, who was a commander in the army of the King of Syria. The bible narrates him to be leper. His name was Naaman. The young girl told her master to go and consult the prophet Elisha about his leprosy. Should he have not listened to him, he would have probably died of his leprosy.

> "[W]here no counsel is, the people fall; but in the multitude of counselors there is safety"
>
> (PROV. 11:14).

God Speaks Through Our Conscience

It is said that your first intuition is never wrong. Have you ever been in a situation where you felt a certain way about a situation but you lacked tangible evidence to back your feeling? Somehow you were confident of your conviction, that is what we call intuition or gut.

Cambridge defines *intuition* as *"unexplained feelings that something is true even when you have no evidence or proof of it."*[8] I believe it is an inner knowing of a situation without any specific data to back it at the time. Have you ever been in a situation or you perceived something but you just could not pin point it? That is your intuition or what we call "gut feeling."

In other words, God has already pre-programmed us to know what we ought to do without imposing on our free will, and He sometimes uses our innate ability to communicate to us when we need guidance.

THE STILL SMALL VOICE

In 1 Kings, we were introduced to a voice of God known as the still small voice:

"And after the earthquake a fire; but the Lord was not in the fire: and after the fire a still small voice"

(1 KINGS 19:12).

The above Scripture is actually the experience of the Prophet Elijah. After he had performed a miracle of letting all the people experience the True God through the sacrifice by fire and executing 400 prophets of Baal. He fled for his life to the wilderness because Jezebel, the queen, threatened to kill him. But he was strengthened by a supernatural food provided by an angel after which God came to him but revealed Himself not in any dramatic way but in a still small voice. I believe that to let us know that sometimes, He may not always talk through thunder and lightning but through the still small voice that we hear in our hearts, that the sounds like whispers are from Him too.

The Lord promises to direct our everyday walk and steps of obedience through His still small voice. This is the voice of whisper of the Holy Spirit as He directs our steps daily. It can manifest itself through sudden inner thoughts, sudden imaginations, or inward visions that we didn't initiate, or through an inspiration generated from a scripture or sudden knowledge or wisdom concerning a direction or decision:

"Roll all your works to God, trust them completely to Him, He will cause your thoughts to be agreeable to His will and then your plans shall prosper and succeed"

(PROV. 16:3 AMP).

Am I the only one jumping out of my seat on that? Even when

you don't know what steps to take, here is what He promises He will do. When you completely give all to Him, and trust Him completely, He will now align your thoughts to be in His will, which means an idea may just pop into your mind as you take that step or through the counsel He gives through the people He has surrounded you with—you will soon discover that it was actually the will of God for you and guess what: those plans will prosper and also succeed.

God Speaks Through Our Process of Transformation

How many times have we heard the phrase, "trust the process"? This is because sometimes God is not giving us a direct answer through words, counsel, or advice from people; it's because He may be speaking about the situation through our daily life processes, working out the little details of our everyday life to conform to the purpose of His will. He may not speak, nonetheless, His watchful eye and foreknowledge of us has already made provision and taken care of the needs required by our purpose and destiny in Christ—this is what we call providence.

UNDERSTANDING THE PROVIDENCE OF GOD

> "I declare the end from the beginning and from ancient times things not yet done, saying 'my counsel shall stand and I will accomplish all my purpose'"

(ISAIAH 46:10).

The word *providence* comes from the Latin word *providentia*, which has two parts: *pro* which means "*forward*," "*on behalf of*" and *vide* which means "*to see with a purpose or to foresee and supply what is needed ahead.*" Hence it denotes "*to make provision for what you see or to supply on behalf of.*"[19][20]

However, providence goes beyond personal to universal. It has everything to do with God's counsel and purpose being accomplished for the entire universe and it's inhabitants; it is the entire universe being in equilibrium, meaning God has already gone ahead of us and established a system to make everything even out according to His purpose. Divine providence is therefore a universal system set up by God "behind the scenes" to aid us in fulfilling our divine mandate by providing the supply needed to make them happen and also allowing us to play our part in the spectra of His global vision.

Therefore, providence shows the scope of God's universal eco system. Think of it as your favorite sports. You're only playing a small part which is being a fan or a spectator. However, it takes a team of players, coaches, cheer leaders, sport agencies, the media, commentators, a stadium and other important vital players to form an athletic organism that we get to call the game of sports. This is how providence looks like; we are only playing a vital part of a universal system in which our contribution and that of other organisms and creations not just humans, equally matter to fulfill the universal purpose of God and also establish His counsel.

The Bible is full of examples of divine providence. One example is when Abraham was about to sacrifice Isaac his son. Before they went up the mountain, Isaac asked his father, "Where is the lamb for the burnt offering?" (Gen. 22:7). Abraham answered, "God will provide for Himself the lamb for the burnt offering, my son" (Gen.

22:8). And when God had shown Abraham a ram caught in the thorns, Genesis 22:14 says, *"Abraham called the name of that place The Lord Will Provide."*

The Hebrew word for *provide* is *raah* which means *"to see."*[21] Hence, Abraham was saying to his son, "God will see for Himself the lamb." And in verse 14: "The Lord will see." Why does God's "seeing" in Hebrew mean that He will provide? Because God's sight always produces purpose. He sees to do something about the situation.

In other words, providence goes beyond foreknowledge to purposeful knowledge. When God "sees," he sees to it; His seeing is always with a view to doing something about the sight. This is the reason why He is called *Jehovah Jireh*, which means *"God who will see to it."*[22]

Remember when Jesus had finished ministering to the multitudes, and they were hungry. None of the adults had food on them, but there was little boy with his lunch: five loaves of bread and two fishes. That wasn't accidental. Jesus knew ahead of time (foreknowledge) that He would be required to feed over 5000 people with food so he sovereignly "saw to it" that there was something tangible enough to perform the miracle. What came into the little boy's mind to bring food along was not a coincidence. God knew the need ahead so He actively provided for it.

Another female example is Queen Esther. She didn't know why she was appointed as Queen until there was a threat to annihilate the Jewish people by their enemy Haman. It was then that her uncle revealed the heart and purpose of why God appointed her in that privilege position:

> "For if you remain completely silent at this time, relief and deliverance will arise for the Jews from another place, but you and your father's house will perish. Yet who knows whether you have come to the kingdom for such a time as this?"

> (EST. 4:14).

You may ask why should you care about the providence of God? Well, the providence of God simply means that God is seeing to it, that He takes care of you even when you don't have a definite blueprint to follow, and you can rest assured that all is well because He has already gone ahead of you and will see to it that everything goes well with you. Even if you miss the mark somehow, everything is working together for your good. Simply put, He's got you!

Therefore, we can rest and trust that in the everyday process of life, He is leading us somewhere, getting us closer daily to our destiny while using us to also solve other people's problems and or meet the needs in our environment. Remember providence goes beyond humans; it sees to it that even the ants are well cared for.

PROVIDENCE ALWAYS MAKES SURE THAT EVERYTHING BALANCES OUT IN DIVINE EQUILIBRIUM.

Perhaps the way to describe providence is through the science of economics. We know that everything is supposed to balance and even out. Likewise, providence is life's economics: everything in nature including the planets, stars, humans, animals, and every system in between including the unseen world have been sovereignly ruled by God to even and balance out in perfect harmony; it is divine government.

God may not answer your prayers right away with step-by-step instructions when you seek Him about your assignment. He may choose to answer it by providence. Thus, trust that He heard you when you asked for His help and know that He is working out everything behind the scenes for you. He will direct your steps. He will put resources around your vicinity and will give you the enlightenment and wisdom to know what to do every step of the way.

Have you bumped into things "coincidentally"? Well, my friend, that was divine providence in action. He knew you would need that resource so He sovereignly saw to it and positioned that there.

Consider the following scripture found in Romans:

> "And we know that all things work together for good to them that love God, to them who are called according to His Purpose"
>
> (ROM. 8:28).

This is the reason why you may have made poor life choices or something really bad has happened to you that should have stopped you from your purpose but it actually helped to get to your destination faster or it enabled you discover your purpose. While the experiences were not pleasant, the lessons in them allowed you to be better prepared for the work that was ahead of you. So, what the enemy meant for harm, God turned it out for your good.

This was the situation with Joseph. After being sold into slavery by his brothers and going through a 13-year process, to becoming the second in command to Pharaoh, he finally understood that the actions of his brothers were beyond personal. Although they meant for harm, God was "seeing" to the greater good of humanity so He sent him to Egypt ahead of time.

In other words, God anticipated the pandemic and thus, made the necessary provision through the leadership of Joseph, which in turn, also preserved Joseph's brothers and their family as well. While they meant evil for him, at the end, their evil acts were used by God to get him closer to his destination of purpose and got him well ahead for preparation of what was to come,

> "but as for you, you meant evil against me, but God meant it for good, in order to bring it about as it is this day; to save many people alive"

(GEN. 50:20).

Judas Iscariot's betrayal of Jesus is also another prime example of providence. After using him to betray Jesus and selling him over, satan thought he had finally gotten rid of Jesus but little did he know that he was actually helping Jesus fulfill His ultimate purpose for humanity : die on the cross and reconciled us back to the Heavenly Father. Therefore scripture makes it clear in 1 Corinthians 2:8 that, *"which none of the rulers of this age knew; for had they known, they would not have crucified the Lord of glory."* That was divine providence in action.

It was the destiny of Jesus to die for humanity but the devil did not know the full scope of God's plans. Therefore, in his attempt to wipe Jesus from the scenes, he had no idea he was being employed by God to help make it happen faster. This even explains why he entered into Judas Iscariot, Jesus told him to speed up the process,

> "Now after the piece of bread, Satan entered him. Then Jesus said to him, "What you do, do quickly"
>
> (JOH. 13:27).

Your enemies are being employed by God through providence to work for you. They may plot and scheme things against you but God will thwart their plans and use it for your good. You may suffer some bruises but you will heal and your scars will serve as a beautiful reminder of God's goodness; your wounds will provide wisdom and those trials and tests will be your testimonies. God is using providence to work everything out for your good.

Trust the Process!

KEY TAKEAWAY: When God gives you assignments, ask questions! God has many ways to answer you: His written word, the Bible, supernatural experiences, through people, intuition, and divine providence. Be open-minded to how He speaks. He does not have one way of relating with us.

6

Mission Possible

"For with God, nothing will be impossible"

—GABRIEL, THE ANGEL (LUKE 1:37 NKJV)

Mission Impossible is an American franchise movie, an action film series in which the main character was an agent of an undercover team from the government known as the Impossible Mission Force. These are a group of highly trained CIA agents from the government who are given undercover assignments known as missions. Their tasks are usually dangerous and look impossible until they are completed. In fact, the main character, played by Tom Cruise, usually goes his own way, sometimes risking his life against authorities to complete the task the IMF have been entrusted with. Hence, the name, Mission Impossible.

While it always looked impossible at first with all the highs and drama, with so many twists and turns, leaving the viewers in suspense, at the end of the movie, the main character would not only overcome the challenges, sometimes with bruises and hurts but would also accomplish the mission.[22]

Likewise, you and I have been entrusted by God with mission(s) that would require certain skill sets and tactics and looked impossible to men, but with God all things are possible.

> "Now the Lord had said to Abram: "Get out of your country, From your family. And from your father's house, To a land that I will show you. I will make you a great nation; I will bless you. And make your name great; And you shall be a blessing. I will bless those who bless you, And I will curse him who curses you; And in you all the families of the earth shall be blessed." So, Abram departed as the Lord had spoken to him, and Lot went with him. And Abram was seventy-five years old when he departed from Haran"
>
> (GEN. 12:1-4 NKJV)

No biblical character's life speaks as heavily on faith as Abraham. The above scripture paints a picture of a real heavenly movie. In this case, the movie is actually about to be the reality of a middle-aged man called Abram who was about to be recruited as an agent in the Impossible Mission Force of Heaven to embark on a mission that would eventually create a legacy of faith and produce an entire nation and through his loins get humanity to be reconciled to God through his seed—the Messiah.

Like the movie, Abram who would later become known as Abraham would have to brace himself for a lifetime adventure with both God, the evolution of his life, and an incredible legacy that would serve as a hallmark for all nations and for all people who would want to have faith in God. He would be forced to confront his fears, face his humanity, and dare to believe in the divine by following God's plan to accomplish the assignment.

Now, there is no way anyone could ever have taken up this challenge without the help of the Holy Spirit. Abraham tried, in my opinion, as a man to take God at His word, and God honored his sacrifice every step of the way.

Scripture relates that when God told him and asked him to sacrifice his comfort zone and leave the place with which he was familiar, Abram obeyed! He left everything, took his wife, his nephew, and a few servants and flocks and headed to a "land that God would show him." Do you realize the vagueness of the instruction? He wasn't giving Abram the actual blueprint or gps.

It's like waking one morning with your clothes packed and heading to the airport with no destination in mind. What do you think people would think of you? First impression: you've lost your mind! But such is the reality of the God we serve; sometimes His instructions are like foolishness to the wisdom of men (1 Cor. 1:25).

Not only that but we also witness many situations where the battle of his flesh as man conflicted with his unwavering faith in God. We will read about his decision to listen to his wife and have a child ahead of God's timing; we will also read about finally giving birth to the promised son, Isaac, and then being tested again to sacrifice his son to God. Then after finally seeing the death of his first wife, for him to remarry and have five more sons. Whew, what a ride!

Sometimes we need to surrender our comfort zones and pleasure for the purpose of God to be established. Whoever told you that obeying God is easy is a big liar. It will cost you to fully yield to His will.Humanity will be forever impacted by Abram's decision to obey God. I wonder what your response to God today would do to your family, your country, and the world.

Whatever God wants to birth through you is intended to live beyond you and outlast. What God gives you is from Him, and it is supposed to leave a lasting legacy for the betterment of humanity. Even after you are dead and gone, many generations are still supposed to benefit from what God used you to birth. Our whole universe is surrounded by architecture and creativity initiated by dead people. Because they chose to build things and or contribute to the lasting impact of humanity, many of these forerunners' names are still been hailed in our times.

So, the next time you celebrate Mother Theresa, Dr. Maya Angelo, Dr. Martin Luther King, Junior, Gandhi, or Nelson Mandela, remember that these were ordinary people who decided to birth their God-given dreams or fight for their convictions. Needless to say, they were daring enough to follow their hearts and today we speak their names with reverence.

If you are ever going to do anything for God, get ready to walk by faith, because God only responds to the language of faith.

What then is faith?

> "Now faith is the assurance (title deed, confirmation) of things hoped for (divinely guaranteed), and the evidence of things not seen [the conviction of their reality—faith comprehends as fact what cannot be experienced by the physical senses]"
>
> **(HEB. 11:1 AMP).**

Let us take for instance the nature of putting things on layaway at your favorite department store in the mall. So you found this cute dress, but you do not have the money to pay for it in full at the stop so you make a deposit to secure your dress with the condition that if you bring the remaining balance you get to keep the stuff. That is what faith can be likened to: putting things on a layaway with the promise of coming back for it with your receipt (the evidence of things not seen).

Thus, faith gives assurance that the things promised in the future are true and you can expect it in the future, hence keep looking forward to it. Faith always produces hope!

The Language of Faith

"All things are possible to them that believe"

(MARK 9:23).

Faith is a conviction based on what you have seen or heard. This is because there is a natural faith in all of us for the things we can see. However, there is also another kind faith, where you haven't physically seen it yet you still believe based on the integrity of the person giving you that promise. This is what Jesus was referring to.

In the Bible, the words faith, believe, and trust all mean the same thing.

One of God's love languages is faith; you prove your love to God by trusting what He says: "But without faith it is impossible to [walk with God and] please Him, for whoever comes [near] to God must [necessarily] believe that God exists and that He rewards those who [earnestly and diligently] seek Him" (Heb. 11:6 AMP).

Faith Versus Fear

The opposite of faith is fear. Whereas faith is the language of God, fear, on the contrary is the language of the devil and it is one of the greatest weapons the enemy uses against Christians. Now I understand that there are natural fears that come with venturing new endeavors just as there are natural faith. However, what we are referring here is the type of fear that cripples you from realizing your dreams and visions, talking you down from responding to God's mandate for you.

The scripture is clear that fear is a spirit (2 Tim. 1:7). However, it is also the very reason the Bible tells us 365 times not to fear; God made sure that every day of the year, we are assured of faith, fear not! When fear grabs you, it paralyzes you, but the truth is that the devil is afraid of you so he does everything to stop you from taking the first step so you don't do anything for God. That way he has already conquered you. But the devil is a liar! Today, God is daring you to rise up and take your rightful place and go after your mandate.

Faith Is Not a Feeling, It Is a Person

"We having the same Spirit of faith, we believe, therefore we speak"

(2 COR. 4:13).

Just as fear is a spirit, faith also has a spirit. His name is the Holy Spirit. When you hang around the Holy Spirit, He emboldens you to believe that all things are possible and therefore you begin to talk like God and act like Him. Allow me to further explain: "[H]ave faith in God" (Mark 11:22).

These were Jesus's response to Peter after he noticed that the fig tree that Jesus had cursed prior had withered, although it did not wither right away.

Theologians believe that this scripture originally means having the God kind of faith. And specifically, to have the God kind of faith, it must come through His Spirit which is imparted by hearing the Word of God.

The more you hang around the Holy Spirit, and hear more and more of God's word, faith is imparted into you. However, it is only through action that you produce the results of faith. Therefore, when Mary encountered the angel and she embraced the Word of God through the angel, faith conceived the seed (Christ) in her.

> "Faith comes by hearing and hearing by the word of God"
>
> (ROM. 10:17 KJV).

When you constantly hang around God's word, it puts faith in you. Quit hanging around people who don't believe in you and who speak words of death because you become what you feed yourself. Start feeding your spirit with God's word: read your Bible daily, listen to anointed sermons, reading anointed books, and constantly listen to life transforming music and guess what—you will be the byproduct of all of these components.

Faith Always Requires Corresponding Action

The best way to illustrate this point is like that of exercise. If you want to build strong muscles, as you much as it may be great to set the goal, register for a gym membership, or hire a personal trainer, until you get to the gym and actually do the work of building the muscles through exercise, your goal or desire to gain the six pack will only remain a wish. If you really want to actual see results, it requires you taking the first step and being consistent over time. Eventually, you will arrive at the desired results. Faith, like muscles, must be exercised in order to produce the results we want.

James 2:14 says *"faith without works is dead,"* which means that whatever dream or vision God has given you, in order to see it manifest, you must do your part by taking the necessary steps to get you started. Sometimes it might mean just acquiring the knowledge about the venture you are intending to pursue. Other times it could mean seeking mentoring, networking opportunities, writing the first sentence etc.—whatever it takes, no matter how big or overwhelmingly impossible it may looked now, your faith in your vision will mean not despising your days of small beginnings; rather it means cultivating what you currently have, trusting that God will take care of the rest.

Now mind you, that does not mean it will be easy, but it will be worth it. I once heard the famous Steve Harvey once say: *"faith does not make it easy; faith makes it possible!"*[23] And with God, you bet you are in for an awesome ride of adventure!

If you are going to fulfill the dream that God has for you, let this understanding be settled in you: you will have to take God at every word He has given you and know that He is everything you will need to manifest His promises if only you will cooperate with Him.

KEY TAKEAWAY: The mandate God gives you may have looked impossible but you have been given faith to shield you backed by His Spirit. As you develop an intimate relationship with Him and feast on His word, nothing will be impossible.

You are not alone

SECTION II

Unveiling #YourSquad

In this section we unveil your gifts of presence. That's right, there are a bunch of people who are for you and have been commissioned by God to help you along every step of your journey to greatness. I call them your squad because they have all been uniquely positioned to play special, individual, or corporate roles in your process of becoming. You might be already conscious of some of them but you are now about to meet some of them too. Either way, it's time to meet your squad, so through them you can leap into the sky! Let's go!

7

God's Got You

"However, apart from Me [cut off from vital union with Me], you can do nothing"

(JOHN 15:5 AMP).

Life is an adventure. No matter the route we choose to take, we are not exempted from troubles. However, how we endure the trials and tests of time is determined by the anchor we hold on to. The famous Comedian and TV Personality, Steve Harvey gave a very powerful motivational speech about God being our anchor:

"During these challenging times, what's really been helpful for me is not these challenging moments but all of my difficult times in my life, is my faith. I've discovered, I'm not the person that I was in my '20s, my '30s, my '40s, I've grown over the years and so have many of you. I was on vacation in Europe last year, I was in Italy. I was on a boat, we were anchored offshore and the captain of the boat was explaining to me why he had anchored in a certain location. And he was saying it was based on the direction of the wind and the swing or the pivot of the boat when it was anchored. When a boat uses or lowers its anchor, he wants the rope or the chain that's attached to the anchor to be long enough to reach the bottom of the ocean or the lake floor. And if it does, the anchor is gonna hold the boat in place so the wind don't blow or push the boat around or the current pushes it into the rocks. Well, while he was talking, I was trippin' because I suddenly realized that God was my anchor and my faith was my chain. I said in the intro that I wasn't who I was in my '20s, my '30s , and my '40s because see back then, my hope was on a short rope. See, so my connection to God was let's just say limited. But back then though I was in much shallower water, so sometimes my anchor could hold me in place when I used it. But, whenever I didn't use my anchor which was my connection to God, even in the little boat in the shallow water, sometimes I'd get tossed. I done even fell out of this boat before and felt like I couldn't even get back up in it. Just like when you fall out of your boat, you get deceived by the evil one who tries to make you think that you ain't gonna do nothing but fall out the boat again, and where was your anchor anyway? Well, to be truthful about it, I wasn't even using it. But the devil was making me think that the anchor didn't work no way, but it does, the only problem is you gotta stay connected to it. So what done happened y'all is, I've gotten older now, I've started to realize that the anchor, my God, always works. I just gotta stay connected to Him. I gotta make sure that my rope and my chain is always attached. And the older you get, the more challenging life becomes, the deeper the water you find yourself in. You ain't in a lake or a river no more, you're in deep water, you're in the ocean. See, the ocean is different, when the wind blow out there on that ocean, it ain't no lake or no river, the wind pick up in the ocean in the deep water that you find yourself in, it creates some waves, huge waves come up, it generates major storms, hurricanes develop out over the ocean, that's where they develop 'cause they're out there in that deep water man, it could get treacherous out here. See, the ocean is so powerful, it can turn over the biggest boat if it's not anchored. Now to anchor out of deep water, your anchor has to get to the ocean floor to hold you steady in this deep water, well guess what? Then you need more chain, you need more faith which is your chain that connects you to your anchor which is God, so he can get to the bottom of things, so he can hold you safe, so he can hold you steady..."[24]

Inspiring speech from Uncle Steve right? I have the same question for you: when the storms of life hit and you have one chance to call for help, who will you call? As a child of God, you can let this truth be settled in your heart: God will NEVER give you an assignment that will not require His involvement to fulfill it! Jesus said in the text above that any meaningful attempt in life without God is "nothing."

Hence, we have the need to know God and how He operates through His Spirit so we can continually yield ourselves to Him and receive the assistance required, not once in a while but all the time.

In this chapter, we shall be focusing on the Holy Spirit as our greatest helper and a key component to fulfilling our God-given dreams.

I love this chapter because here, you get to be re-introduced to your greatest cheerleader. The one who loves you the most, is crazy about you and will always be present to help you—God, the Holy Spirit.

I am confident that by the inspiration of the Holy Spirit from this book, your faith will be stirred up, and you will receive the boldness to say, *"I can do all things through Christ that strengthens me"* (Phil. 4:13). In other words, through the Spirit of God in your life.

So, let's get started!

Meet God, the Holy Spirit

It's important to state at this point that we have only one God—*"Hear, O Israel: The LORD our God is ONE LORD"* (Deut. 6:4). But our God exists in three persons: God the Father, God the Son (Jesus), and God the Holy Spirit. This three-fold existence is called the Trinity. We will be examining the third person of the Trinity in this chapter.

To begin with, the third person of the Trinity, the Holy Spirit didn't just appear like a stray missile. He was first mentioned during creation in the third verse of the first chapter of Genesis, the first book of the Bible. He was one of the key players during creation. It was evident that the creation of the earth and all that is in it was a collaborative effort by the Trinity. No wonder the creation is so perfect such that no technological advancement has attempted to duplicate the re-creation of the earth.

The Holy Spirit is also referred to as the Spirit of God in Genesis 1:2, hovering over the waters while the earth was still without form, void, and dark. He came into the scene and covered the waters; He came upon the chaotic scene, and creation started.

Likewise, if we are ever going to create something that will outlive us or something that will expand the Kingdom of God, we need the help of the Holy Spirit. He has to also hover over us to help us birth it out. We can never do anything for God without His Spirit.

In Luke chapter 1, we saw an instance where angel Gabriel appeared to Mary to tell her about the birth of Jesus. She was going to conceive and birth a *"Holy One."* But for that to take place, see what the angel said in verse 35, *"And the Angel answered her, 'The Holy Spirit will come upon you, and the power of the Most High will overshadow you; therefore the child to be born will be called holy—the Son of God.'"* So we see that the Holy Spirit is that force that overshadows a man to birth God's plan on the earth. Hallelujah!

We need the Holy Spirit to carry out any divine assignment on the earth. He is like a lubricant that makes the work easy and smooth. God does not desire that we struggle in life. When Jesus was about to leave the earth, in other to allay the fear of His Disciples, He started talking to them about another comforter, someone who would be with them permanently. In John chapter 14, He introduced them to the Holy Spirit. He said he would not leave them without the helper and comforter. The task ahead was a huge one. But He had just the person for the job, the Holy Spirit.

He was going to make sure that the apostles were successful at every turn. Zechariah 4:6 says, *"it's not by might, nor by power but by my Spirit...."* Everything God does is done and controlled by the Holy Spirit, and in verse 10 of John 14, Jesus had told them, the Father in me, He does the works. Jesus taught His disciples to pray to the Father in heaven, but here Jesus says there's the Father that dwells in Him who is doing all the works they see. He was revealing a mystery.

GENTLE AND PEACEFUL

One amazing attribute of the Holy Spirit is gentleness and quietness. He is a peaceful Spirit. God the Father declared in Genesis 6:3, *"My Spirit shall not always strive with man..."* in other words, the Spirit of God will not struggle with man to do anything. He is here to help but will not force His way into anyone.

Jesus emphasized this truth in Luke 11:13. He said that the Holy Spirit is the promise of God to man. And the Father is willing to give the Holy Spirit to only those who *"ask."* If you lack the help of the Holy Spirit in your life, it's because you have not asked or invited Him.

Similarly, one of the fruits of the Holy Spirit is gentleness. This shows that we can live a gentle and quiet life amid chaos because we have a gentle Spirit in us.

SENSITIVE

This is also another attribute or nature of the Holy Spirit. Sensitivity is when one has the tendency to be easily hurt or has the capacity to be aware of the needs as well as the emotions of others. Believe me, this definition is typical of the Holy Spirit. He is a person, and so He knows how you feel. He can tell when you need His help, He knows your weaknesses, and He can supply the strength you need to pull through.

On the other hand, Ephesians 4:30 says, *"do not grieve the Holy Spirit of God."* In other words, He has emotions also and can be grieved or hurt whenever we do the wrong thing.

THE SPIRIT OF TRUTH

In John 14:17, Jesus introduced the Holy Spirit to His disciples as the Spirit of truth. His role in the lives of believers is to guide them into all truth. It is through the Spirit of God that we can know the truth of God's Word and also keep away from errors and mistakes.

THE SPIRIT OF HOLINESS

"And declared to be the Son of God with power, according to the spirit of holiness, by the resurrection from the dead"
(ROM. 1:4).

The Holy Spirit is equally referred to as the Spirit of holiness. It is not just hard to live holy but impossible to live a holy life without the help of the Spirit of God. By this attribute, He helps us to separate from an unclean thing so we can please God.

THE SPIRIT OF WISDOM

"That the God of our Lord Jesus Christ, the Father of glory may give unto you the spirit of wisdom and revelation in the knowledge of him"
(EPH. 1:17).

The Holy Spirit imparts within us the ability to operate in a higher dimension of supernatural wisdom, which is different from the intellectual wisdom and common sense. Joseph was able to interpret the dream of Pharaoh and proffer a solution to a national problem by the wisdom of God imparted in him by the Holy Spirit. Even Pharaoh, King of Egypt, exclaimed, *"Can we find such a one as this is, a man in whom the Spirit of God is?"* (Gen. 41:38). What an extraordinary life.

Furthermore, the greatest event in a man's life is the salvation of his soul from the kingdom of darkness into the kingdom of light. But even salvation requires the help of the Holy Spirit. Jesus said He is the person that convicts a man of his sin. The Bible says, *"and no one can say, 'Jesus is Lord,' except by the Holy Spirit"* (1 Cor. 12:3).

I can go on and on telling you about the Holy Spirit. Understand that, our sweet Holy Spirit is not a vague, or an impersonal force.

Neither is He an "It," a concept, nor a mystical impression. He is a person, a true friend, and the greatest companion in the journey of life. Meet the third person in the Trinity.

You've Got the Power!

"The Holy Ghost shall come upon thee, and the power of the Highest shall overshadow thee: therefore, also that holy thing which shall be born of thee shall be called the Son of God"

(LUKE 1:35).

There are times in life when we see our inadequacies and inability right before us. In fact, there are moments when we disqualify ourselves from God's call over our lives because we think we are not able. Well, over and again I have seen God using the less qualified and empowering them to carry out great tasks. God always pours His treasures in *"earthen vessels."* Isaiah 40:29 says, *"He gives power to the weak. He increases the strength of him who has no might."* So, you have the power!

Now let's learn again from Mary, the mother of Jesus. Mary had not yet experienced salvation, but Jesus, the Savior, was coming to live within her, so she got to be the first person to experience what it is like to have Jesus live within you. And for her, it was not just by the Spirit, but she gets to also experience God, the Son, as a baby, physically moving in her body.

In all honesty, while it may look as if she was the one carrying Jesus, from the Creator's point of view, her very life was being carried by the Savior in her womb. Life was living within her. The Word that formed the entire universe and made her in His image and likeness was being reincarnated at the place of her obedience.

The little Jewish maiden believed God but couldn't imagine what the angel described. It was too much for her mind to bear. Mary asked, *"how shall these things be?"* Now, you have to understand that she wasn't asking if it was possible. She was asking how it would be made possible.

She was a virgin, and she knew how people got pregnant. But she was about to be introduced to the person of the Holy Spirit. The angel said to her, "the Holy Spirit shall come upon her."

He was saying in essence, *"God, the Holy Spirit, will make it happen. He is both God and the power of God."* Yes! The Holy Spirit is the power of the highest the angel was talking about. He makes all God's purposes become a reality by His power.

Friend, I want to show you that the Holy Spirit doesn't just have power, He is power! He is the very embodiment of God's power. Understand that, anytime God commissions us for an assignment, He also provides His power via His Spirit to enable us to fulfill it.

Jesus emphasized this truth when He assured His disciples of one of the primary purposes of the Holy Spirit in our lives. He said in Acts 1:8, *"Ye shall receive power after that the Holy Ghost has come upon you."* Can you see the power in relation to the Holy Spirit here again? Consider this: power was to come to them when the Holy Ghost arrived. They could only have this power when His presence came upon them.

The Nine Gifts of the Holy Spirit

The presence of the Holy Spirit signifies the arrival of the power of God. And power is defined as the ability to perform a task. So, we have the Nine gifts of the Holy Spirit, which are the various supernatural abilities of the Holy Spirit in us. In other words, they are the various ways through which we manifest the power of God not for showing off but to be a blessing to humanity, especially to the body of Christ.

The Spirit has given each of us a special way of serving others. Some of us can speak with wisdom, while others can speak with knowledge, but these gifts come from the same Spirit.

To others, the Spirit has given great faith or the power to heal the sick or the power to work mighty miracles. Some of us are prophets, and some of us recognize when God's Spirit is present. Others can speak different kinds of languages, and still others can tell what these languages mean.

But it is the Spirit who does all this and decides which gifts to give to each of us (1 Cor. 12:7-11 KJV, author's paraphrase).

Now let me let you in briefly on these gifts.

THE WORD OF KNOWLEDGE

God has total knowledge of all things, but we are limited in knowledge of even what goes on around us. The word of knowledge is the ability of the Holy Spirit to transmit some specific information or knowledge of something that you may not know by your own limited intelligence or level of knowledge, e.g., knowledge of how to start a business or how to solve a problem at work, among others.

THE WORD OF WISDOM

Wisdom is the correct application of knowledge. This is like a step further from the word of knowledge. There are times when the knowledge is enough to solve the issue, while at other times, you need the word of wisdom to properly apply the knowledge you have. For instance, Joseph appeared before and was told about a dream the King had. How would he interpret the dream to address real life issues?

THE GIFT OF PROPHECY

"But one who prophesies speaks to men for edification and exhortation and consolation"

(1 COR. 14:3).

This gift is the ability to receive a direct word from God on behalf of somebody else or a group of people. It is given primarily to edify, exhort and console. It is important to note that the gift of Prophecy is different from the office of the Prophet. A prophet is an individual called into the five-fold ministerial office. Ephesians 4:7-11 is clear that the prophetic office is Christ's gift to the Body of Christ : *"But to each one of us grace was given according to the measure of Christ's gift. ... And He gave some as apostles, and some as prophets, and some as evangelists, and some as pastors and teachers."*

Therefore, just because an individual can prophesy does not make them a prophet. Actually, we are all encouraged to desire to prophesy by the Apostle Paul : *"Pursue love, yet desire earnestly spiritual gifts, but especially that you may prophesy. For one who speaks in a tongue does not speak to men but to God; for no one understands, but in his spirit he speaks mysteries. But one who prophesies speaks to men for edification and exhortation and consolation"* (1 Cor. 14:1-3).

God wants us to earnestly pursue all His gifts especially the gift of prophecy so we can encourage each other to stand firm in our walk with Him. As a child of God, you need to be *"prophetic"* because the Holy Spirit lives in you.

However, it is the Holy Spirit who determines who He appoints into the office of the prophet.

THE GIFT OF FAITH

The Bible says, *"For by grace are ye saved through faith..."* (Eph. 2:8). That is, every believer has a measure of faith at salvation, and our Christian adventure is totally by faith. Men with the gift of faith display extraordinary confidence and boldness. They talk about *"when"* something will happen and not *"if"* it happens. Some situations confront us that our faith may not doubt the possibility of a way out. But this divine ability makes us move forward when others turn back.

THE GIFT OF HEALING

Jesus said we shall lay hands on the sick, and they shall recover. That means every believer can manifest this gift. There are a lot of people around who need healing, and the Holy Spirit wants to empower us to pray for them and God heals them.

THE WORKING OF MIRACLES

Miracles are supernatural phenomena that transcend natural laws. In other words, they are occurrences that have no natural explanation, e.g., Jesus turning water to wine, and multiplied five loaves of bread and two fishes to feed 5000 people. The Bible is filled with diverse miracles wrought by the power of God. And God desires to still do the same today. Jesus said we shall do greater work. And this means this gift is needed to perform such jaw-dropping signs even today.

THE DISCERNMENT OF SPIRITS

We are living in a deceptive season when all kinds of spirits are manifesting in people and manipulating others. So, the Holy Spirit will empower believers to be able to discern the happenings behind the scene at every instance. Many people are oppressed by demonic spirits or human spirits, but with this gift, even the spirits pretending to be for God will be exposed.

DIFFERENT KINDS OF TONGUES

This is simply the Holy Spirit giving you the ability to speak languages that you naturally can't speak. For instance, you are Chinese, and he gives you the ability to speak French or Spanish. Also, he can give you the "heavenly tongue," which the Bible calls the tongue of angels in 1 Corinthians 13.

THE INTERPRETATION OF TONGUES

Most people with the gift of different kinds of tongues sometimes don't understand what they are saying, especially if its heavenly language. There is the need for another ability of the Holy Spirit to interpret what is being said. It can either be in a church where you can interpret another person's tongue or the Holy Spirit giving you the ability to interpret your own tongue.

Now, if you study the gospels, you'll see that Jesus operated in these gifts of the Holy Spirit. The good news is that this is the same Spirit in Jesus that is in all believers. The Holy Spirit was the one who made Jesus powerful, and Jesus said that he who believes in Him would do the works that He did and even greater works. That is, works greater in scope and magnitude.

Guess what! You can also connect to any of these gifts and operate in it, but it begins with a desire. Yes, you have to desire the gifts. Paul said, *"I want you to desire the best gifts..."* (I Cor. 12:31). Then you need to stir up that gift. Paul reminded his son Timothy of this in 2 Timothy, saying, *"For this cause, I remind you that you should stir up the gift of God which is in you..."* (2 Tim. 1:6 WEB).

Just like you may not enjoy the sweetness of a cup of tea with sugar in it if you fail to stir it after adding the sugar, so is the gift of God in you if not stirred. The world is waiting for your manifestation. You already have the power through the Holy Spirit, so stir it! Express it! And watch your life glow as God desires.

Growing in Character

"But the fruit of the Holy Spirit (the work which his presence within accomplishes) is love, joy (gladness), peace, patience (an even temper, forbearance), kindness, goodness (benevolence), faithfulness, gentleness (meekness, humility), self-control (self-restraint, continence). Against such things, there is no law [that can bring a charge]"

(GAL. 5:22-23 AMP).

Apart from gifts, the Holy Spirit also develops spiritual fruit in the life of the believer. The "fruit of the Holy Spirit" refers to the nature of the Spirit revealed in the life of the believer, the spiritual qualities which should be evident in the lives of all Christians. The truth is, God's ultimate aim for us as His children is for us to be sanctified and acceptable before Him, and part of that sanctification process is the Holy Spirit transmitting that divine nature and likeness of God into us. That is His work.

To be Christ-like is to be like Christ in character. A character like a stature must be projected. People should see it when they interact with you.

They say your gifts will make room for you, but it is your character that will keep you where you are. When it comes to working for God, character is very much an important component as the execution of the vision itself. In Matthew 7:21–23, Jesus emphasized this truth by saying that on the last day, many will come forth displaying their gifts, but because they lack the fruits, they will still be cast out of His sight.

Our character is an integral part of our purpose in God. The Bible reveals that believers have been predestined by God to be conformed to the image of Christ, and 1 John 2:6 tells us that we are to live as Jesus lived. Friend, we can only live as Jesus lived if we have His character.

But we can only have His character by the fruit of the Spirit, because just as the gifts are to make us like Jesus in power, the fruit is to make us like Jesus in character. The gifts empower us to do, but the fruit empowers us to be.

Someone said, "character is who you are when no one is around." It is the ability to fulfill purpose unsupervised. Character is inner strength and purity. It's the stuff that makes an authentic person. Without character, you can't keep or sustain what you've built over the years. Lack of character will make you destroy all your achievements.

It's important to state here that everyone has character, which can be developed overtime. However, you can either have a godly character (through the help of the Holy Spirit) or a stinking character.

A man without a godly character can be likened to a pig. Even if a pig is cleaned and wears a lovely bow, when no one is watching, the pig would waddle back into the mud and make futile all efforts to keep it clean. Believe me, friend, even in relationships, your character is needed to keep any meaningful relationship. No one wants to hang around stench!

Furthermore, your power, charisma, or charm might bring people around, but your character will keep them or send them off. Ecclesiastes 10:1 says, "Dead flies cause the ointment of the apothecary to send forth a stinking savor: so doth a little folly [in] him that is in reputation for wisdom and honor." Wow! Even the smallest character flaw can damage a good reputation. Think about this!

Therefore, my question to you is, do you have a godly character? Is integrity a standard you live by? Do you lie to get your way, or maybe you often exaggerate a little? Do you make promises you can't keep? Do you breach agreements, or break trust, or mismanage funds? Are you honest with others and with yourself? Can people depend on you? Are you truthful?

The fruit of the Spirit is the character of God, and He is much more concerned about us walking in His character than working for Him. He is interested in molding us daily to express the image of Christ through the fruit of the Spirit.

"For whom He foreknew, he also predestinated to be conformed into the image of His son..."

(ROM. 8:29 KJV).

How then can you grow in the Fruit of the Spirit? COME TO THE SOURCE!

God is the source of these fruits. You must first take a step unto salvation. That is, renounce sin and allow the life of God to flow through you. Jesus said in John, "Every branch in me that does not bear fruit he takes away, and every branch that does bear fruit he prunes that it may bear more fruit" (John 15:2 ESV). In other words, one major reason for being in Christ is to bear fruit. You must first abide in the vine, connect to the root, which is God, then the nutrient to bear fruit will flow. Also, be filled with the Holy Spirit. Pray for a baptism of the Spirit of God.

RELY ON THE HOLY SPIRIT

Growing in the fruit of the Spirit cannot be achieved by mere determination. It's not a New Year's resolution. It requires the help of the Holy Spirit. Zechariah says, *"Not by might, nor by power, BUT BY MY SPIRIT, saith the LORD of hosts"* (Zech. 4:6 emphasis added). Without the help of the Holy Spirit, you will just struggle to be patient with people or even love or forgive them. The Bible says, "God is working in you to make you willing and able to obey him." So, rest in His help, not your human ability.

DISPLAY THE FRUIT

"Exercise Yourself Toward Godliness"

(1 TIM. 1:7 WEB)

To emerge a star in athletics, regular exercise is not an option. The same with the fruit of the Spirit. As the Holy Spirit is working in you and showing you from the word of God or admonitions from other believers, begin to take steps. A child that will run must first toddle. For instance, even if you were not as patient as you expect, don't be hard on yourself and don't give up either. Keep at it! Live each day in the consciousness of bearing the fruit of the Spirit, and gradually, you will keep growing unto perfection.

Jesus is our light! Let your light so shine before men that they would see your good works (Matt. 5:16). Do you see it? Godly Character brings about good works. Let's walk in love, be patient with those around you. Treat people how Christ would treat them. *"By this, you show the world that you are the Son of your Father in Heaven"* (Matt. 5:45).

God, The Majority

"If God be for us, who can be against us"

(ROM. 8:31 KJV).

I went into details about the Holy Spirit to assure you that once you have the third person of the Trinity on your side, there is absolutely nothing you cannot do. If you have no one but God, He's all you need because God alone is a Majority!

A lot of us make mistakes when we receive an idea or an instruction from God, and we tend to assume that our family and close loved ones are required to support us. Then, if we don't get their support, we tend to feel discouraged and feel we can't do it; if many of us are honest with ourselves, we will rightly say we get our feelings hurt and become offended. But it shouldn't be!

Truth is, while it's great to vouch for their unwavering support, your friends and loved ones are not your target market; they are not under any obligation to buy your products, finance your dreams, or cheer you on. If they do it, awesome, but if they don't, it doesn't mean the dreams can't be materialized without them.

When you have God on your side, He will cause you to soar and do exploits by His Power and provide all the resources and even strangers to support you (more about this in the coming chapter). Don't be afraid or discouraged if the closest people around you don't get it, they are not meant to. Sometimes too, their involvement might be a big distraction or a hindrance from trusting God all the way.

Sometimes all God wants to do is show off His power, but if people are in the way, how can you see the salvation and power of God. No wonder John the Baptists said, *"I must decrease that He may increase"* (Joh 3:30).

Let go of yourself, allow God to increase His nature and power in you, agree with Him today, and see how meaningful and fulfilling your life can be.

Your God-given dream is a reality already. Connect with God and watch yourself soar higher.

KEY TAKEAWAY: God, the Holy Spirit is your first gift of presence. His abiding presence is always with you, as long as you have received Jesus as your Lord and personal Savior, and He is ready to work with you to do exploits for Jesus. Step up with confidence because He is with you and for you.

8

Embracing Your Mentors

> "Now indeed, Elizabeth your relative has also conceived a son in her old age; and this is now the sixth month for her who was called barren"
>
> (LUKE 1:36).

I'd liken Elizabeth to a gold mine. This is because she is an important component who will foster the progression and growth of Mary in her process of becoming the mother of Jesus with her wisdom and mentoring.

Although God was going to do His part by implanting the seed in her womb, God was not all that Mary needed to birth Jesus and raise Him for the purpose He had been given on this earth. It would require human involvement; a key component was going to come through some important roles certain people were going to play for the overall spectacle of God's plan through Jesus for humanity.

We would not have known the importance of a human factor until the angel channeled Mary's focus to her cousin, Elizabeth, who apparently was pregnant in her old age. Dive with me for a moment and let's study together about the golden Elizabeth.

We were first introduced to her as the wife of the priest,

Zachariah. He faithfully served God in the temple and one day, encountered the angel Gabriel about the birth of their son in their old age (Read the entire passage of Luke 1). According to the narrative, Zachariah was made dumb until their son was born to prevent him from jeopardizing the plan of God concerning the boy who would later grow up to be known as John the Baptist and would "prepare the way of the Lord." John later baptized Jesus for His earthly ministry.

Biologically, Elizabeth was the older cousin of Mary. Therefore, there was already an established relationship that was about to be further nurtured in birthing the prophetic promise.

Why is it that of all millions of people in the world at the time, God handpicked her above all women? Because what Mary was about to birth was related to what Elizabeth was carrying.

Understanding the Process of Becoming

> "There is Nothing New Under the Sun"
> —KING SOLOMON (ECCL. 1:9).

As much as what Mary was about to bear was new and was going to revolutionize the world, the experience of birthing was not new. Whatever God will birth through you, as long as it is under the sun, it has happened before! From the beginning of humanity till now, some things have repeated, but changes in their delivery and dynamism depend on the generation and the times when they are meeting those needs.

For example, every biological mother has experienced the process of pregnancy, yet each mother, regardless of the times they become a mother, goes through a unique experience with their pregnancy. However, the process is still the same everywhere as the universal law states that the only way to have a baby is through the womb, although there have been few exceptions.

Therefore, while what you carry may be new, someone, somewhere on this earth right now, has or is going through it, and their lessons may be necessary for your success and survival, without the pain and bruises.

Experience, they say, is the best teacher. This is the reason the Bible has numerous examples in both the old and the new testaments. From Moses and Joshua, Elijah and Elisha, Eli and Samuel to Jesus and His disciples, these are just a few of the people who imparted knowledge, skill, anointing and influence to their protégés.

Understanding the Power of Mentorship

It is crucial to realize that although there were a lot of more prestigious women, probably younger, prettier, educated, and financially secured, still, God handpicked Elizabeth because of what Mary was about to experience—the birth of Jesus, the long-awaited Messiah. Elizabeth had some golden nuggets for her that could determine the destiny of the baby she carried. So yes, she was an older woman getting pregnant for the first time, which probably was weird given the circumstances surrounding her pregnancy, but it is also the very reason she was the right person to help Mary because what Mary also carried was also going to put her in a similar category of weirdness.

Although the Holy Spirit will incubate the seed, Elizabeth's role in Mary's life would determine whether she keeps or aborts what she carried. In other words, who you hang around with will determine how fast or slow, productive or abortive, you become towards your purpose and God's dream for your life.

Elizabeth's husband encountered the same angel that Mary encountered; thus, to some extent, she was currently in Mary's shoes, hearing a prophetic promise from God and holding on to it until it materialized. Mary needed Elizabeth to withstand the test of time, the trials of her faith, and the birthing of Jesus. Never underestimate the potential power of an Elizabeth in your life. This is what we call the art of mentorship!

WHO IS YOUR ELIZABETH?

Mentoring is a very powerful and transformative system that can take any inexperienced person into a place of power when done right, and it yields innumerable benefits that outlast both the mentee and the mentor. According to the Webster Dictionary, a *mentor* is simply defined as *"a trusted counselor or guide."*[25]

Therefore, the right mentor's role in your life is to simply counsel and guide you in the way you should go in the direction of your goals and dreams.

From this definition, we can also say that a mentor is anyone who serves as a voice of reason, who coaches, offers emotional support, or is a trusted resource for your mandate. They are usually people who have either charted the path or have traveled on the road or even climbed the ladder to the dreams that you are about to embark on, with valuable lessons from the wins, losses, pains, and gains.

The Bible emphasized the importance and benefits of mentorship when it instructed us to *"train up a child in the way he should go so that when they grow, they will not depart from it"* (Prov. 22:6 NKJV).

While a lot of people have taken this to apply to just biological parenting, I believe the Bible's multifaceted abilities to speak to every area of our development make this scripture also apply to our development and birthing of our God-given commissions. Therefore, this scripture is an instruction to anyone in a position to influence a child's life. A child in this context does not necessarily mean a biological child but any inexperienced person who is sitting at a place of a child.

A mentor in this context is a parent or instructor who has custody of a child. This scripture is, therefore, instructing such a person to "*train up*" that child "*in the way he should go"* so he can produce the outcome, *"so when he grows, he won't depart from it."*

Now, let's go deeper into this:

To *train* means "*to teach a particular skill or type of behavior through practice and instruction over a period of time so as to make fit, qualified or productive to form by instruction, discipline or drill.*"[26]

Therefore, the Bible is saying that a mentor's primary role is to:

1. Teach
2. Instruct
3. Discipline

until it becomes the second nature of the protégé to mature in the way they are supposed to go.

A child in this context refers to an inexperienced person. Normally, we know that children by nature are very naïve, so they do childish things, which sometimes requires discipline and instructions to get them aligned.

Therefore, a protégé is likened to a child, sitting at a feet of a parent, receiving the instructions, counseling, precepts, and disciplines in the direction of their purpose, so they can become a confident, competent, and highly skilled (matured) individual who is firmly grounded on the principles instilled in them, which then serve as guideposts so they can succeed in their endeavors. This, I believe, is the power of mentorship!

Hence, it is the primary duty of your mentor to provide an insider's vision that they are trying to birth through the lens of their own life experiences, lessons, and mistakes they have made along the way in the journey of their own process of becoming. It is also the primary responsibility of the protégé to behave like a child and have a teachable spirit so the mentor can pour into them and train them in the way they should go.

Depending on the nature of mentorship, sometimes, the protégé gets to work in the close proximity of the mentor for some time like that of Mary and Elizabeth. Mary had to move in with Elizabeth and stay with her for three months to learn crucial lessons, which would be very instrumental in her sustenance of both her pregnancy, the birthing, and the raising of the Son of God.

FOUR SIGNS THAT YOU HAVE MET YOUR ELIZABETH

It has been proven time and time again that when someone receives mentorship, in whatever area of calling, gifting, expertise, talent, or skill, they excel far greater than their counterparts.

Therefore, whatever vision or prophetic promise you receive from God, you need a mentor to help you accomplish it if you want to reach your fullest potential. So, what are the signs that you have met your Elizabeth? Well, here are key principles we can learn from Mary and Elizabeth's dynamic mentoring relationship:

- *God Appointed Elizabeth*

It was the angel that brought Mary's mind to Elizabeth. She didn't choose her. This is crucial. As much as there may be many competent and more skillful or favorable people you would prefer, you don't choose your mentors; God does! He alone knows what He has deposited in you and also uniquely invested in them for them to pour into your unique calling.

- *The Baby in Her Leaped When She Met Mary At the appearance of Mary on the scene, the baby in Elizabeth kicked (Luke 1:41–44).*

This is because what was in Elizabeth (John) was connected to what was in Mary's womb (Jesus). John was going to grow up to pave the way for Jesus's ministry. When you meet your Elizabeth, what is in you will connect with what is in them. There will be some instant spiritual chemistry, where you will both know that you are destined for each other.

- *She Confirmed Mary's Prophetic Destiny Just Like the Angel Had Said*

Elizabeth strengthened the faith of Mary right away when she also began to declare the same blessings on Mary, as spoken by the angel: *"then she spoke out with a loud voice and said, 'Blessed are you among women, and blessed is the fruit of your womb'"* (Luke 1:42 NKJV).

Your mentors will confirm what God has already spoken in the spirit about you. This is vital! When you meet your Elizabeth, they will not speak anything contrary to what God has already spoken concerning you and your dreams. This is also a clear indicator because their confirmation is supposed to serve as God's endorsement of you. Anything outside of that is a distraction. God didn't say you are to hype them; they are to affirm your prophetic mandate according to the blueprint of heaven.

- ### *She Encouraged Mary and Nurtured What Was in Her for Three Months*

Mary stayed with Elizabeth for three months and learned the process of pregnancy from her. Elizabeth's situation was unique in the sense that she became pregnant in her old age; she probably had gone through some ridicule and also experienced all the symptoms that Mary was about to go through, yet she was strong and had faith in God. These were salient lessons that Mary had to learn from her older cousin. When you meet the right mentors, they may allow you close proximity, which I strongly advise you take full advantage of it because they don't usually last. Mary's mentorship lasted three months; mine lasted seven years.

Yours might last two years or more or less, depending on what your vision or dream from God is and the process of your mentorship. But no matter how long the process lasts, these pointers remain—they will encourage and show you the secrets to success. They may allow you to peek into their private lives, seeing at first hand their personal failures so you don't repeat those mistakes and will also give you a glimpse into their wins. Sometimes, they may share their wins with you too, so that you can know it is possible.

So, my question to you today is: who are your mandate mentors? Are they nurturing what you are carrying or killing it? Ideally, the right mentor for you will always be excited for you because they understand the power of legacy—what you carry is directly tied to theirs, and should you succeed, it always goes into their credit. However, we understand that sometimes that is not the case. Nonetheless if they miss it along the way, God will still compensate you for doing the right thing and submitting to their leadership.

May the Lord lead you to the right mentors for your destiny.

KEY TAKEAWAY: Dreams or visions from God always benefit greatly from successful mentorships. Don't cut the potential of what you carry by neglecting this powerful system ordained by God to help you succeed in your life mandate.

9

Your Silent Heroes

We live in a time when everyone wants to be known. In fact, the days when people used to do things privately have become the things of the past. But I'd like for us to celebrate important figures who played vital roles in the life of Mary and Jesus without bringing the limelight to themselves, nonetheless their roles and marks can never be erased: Joseph (the earthly father of Jesus), Simeon (the priest), and Anna (the prophetess)!

The Gift of Joseph

As we know it, Joseph was quite an interesting character when it comes to his role in the birthing of Jesus and his well-being. We all know that according to the biblical account, he was the fiancé of Mary, a young man who was a descendant of David. Little is known about him until after Jesus was born, and we later found out that he was a carpenter by profession.

Perhaps what even makes his story more interesting lies in the fact that little was said about him after the birth of Jesus in the four gospels with the exception that he married Mary and took the boy as his earthly son and provided for Him. However, after the incident of the young Jesus found in the temple preaching, there was no account of Joseph, the earthly father of Jesus, anymore. What happened to him?

Well, we are about to find out!

THE DESCENDANT OF DAVID

Scriptures describe Joseph as being the seed of David (Matt. 1:20), which means he is from the tribe of Judah and also Mary's fiancé. When he found out that Mary was pregnant, he wanted to break their engagement privately because obviously, he didn't believe her story that it was the Holy Spirit who did that to her. Being an honorable man, he didn't want to publicly humiliate and endanger Mary's life because, according to their customs at the time, if a woman were found pregnant without first being married, she could be stoned to death (Deut. 22:13-21). So, he intended and planned in his heart to end things with Mary quietly when God intervened by sending an angel to appear to him in a dream, saying *"Joseph, Son of David, do not be afraid to take Mary as your wife for that which is conceived in her is by the Holy Ghost"* (Matt. 1:20).

It is interesting how Mary hurriedly embraced the mandate to become the mother of Jesus without considering the cost of her loss. Remember, she hadn't consulted with Joseph before accepting God's offer from the angel; she was willing to lose her marriage so she could go through the shame of birthing the prophetic promise.

However, God went ahead of her and sorted out any potential mess and threats to her life and what she was carrying and to also secure her covering. This is a vital lesson we all need to take note of. When the Lord commissions us to do something for Him, we must be willing to fully go out and trust Him to sort out all the little details about how the process will play out.

Now, back to Joseph. Take an imaginative exercise with me for a moment, and let's imagine what it would have been like for Joseph to have to accept the birthing of another child that is not his seed and love and provide and protect the child as his own. Mind you also, that in those days, there was nothing like blended family; it's either you're a biological child or product of a concubine. A woman didn't have a lot of options, and for a betrothed woman like Mary, you might as well say your last prayers because it is likely you would be stoned to death. But Joseph embraced the challenge and gave himself wholly to it, by accepting the call to become the loving husband of this young lady and also the earthly father of the Son of God.

That, in my opinion, is the greatest calling and the highest privilege because how do you father God?

A DOTTING HUSBAND & FAMILY MAN

As a husband to Mary, Joseph has to play husband duties to his wife by providing the nurturing, love, and support that every wife requires of her husband.

Also, with respect to being an adoptive earthly father of Jesus, he had to see Mary daily, with all the pregnancy symptoms and bodily changes. He also has to endure everything, including the mood swings, and still be gracious and loving her through it all.

Furthermore, life after the birth of Jesus would see Joseph lovingly provide for his wife through all the seasons of life.

A CONSISTENT SPIRITUAL MAN

> "His parents went to Jerusalem every year at the Feast of the Passover. And when He was twelve years old, they went up to Jerusalem according to the custom of the feast"
>
> (LUKE 2: 41-42)

This scripture gives us a glimpse of the spiritual life of Joseph. Every year, he led his family to worship God and fulfill their rites of worship. God knew He could trust Joseph with His son because any man who is consistent in his devotion to God is capable of raising a solid family that fears the Lord. Joseph proved that. He did not just send his family and stay home; he went with them.

A LOVING FATHER

As a father, Joseph not only became the adopted earthly father of Jesus, but he also had other biological children with Mary. His fatherly duties not only included providing food, clothing, and shelter in his home. He also had to provide the right spiritual atmosphere for his family and Jesus. Joseph had to make sure he taught him the way of the Lord. Because of his stability and guidance, Jesus was provided for, fed, and nurtured.

HE HAD A FAMILY BUSINESS

As a responsible man, Joseph was very industrious, and he had a family business. The Bible relates that he was a carpenter; thus, Jesus became a carpenter (Mark 6:3; Matt. 13:55). Jesus started working with his father, Joseph, as an apprentice, a direct protégé of his father, and Joseph skillfully trained Him to become a professional who later ran his father's business.

As a result, Jesus was not left to fend for himself. Although He was God, He came as a human, and with the human living experiences he built upon the foundations that his earthly father laid for him to soar into greater altitudes. Hence, Jesus grew in wisdom and stature, and in favor with both God and men (Luke 2:52) because He had a godly role model set before him through his earthly father.

HE WAS A MAN OF CHARACTER

Joseph was a man of character. Nothing notorious was said about him. Because of his covering, Jesus grew up in a stable home, free of scandals. Little is said about him other than the fact that he was "the carpenter's son" (Matt. 13:55). Joseph was not self-seeking because he understood that no matter how high Jesus might climb in the ladder of success and fame, He would always be the "carpenter's son."

Yes, He is the Son of God, and even God Himself, but when it comes to His human relation, His glory was dependent on Joseph's success in raising Him up for His earthly assignment and also being sustained in character that usually outlasts anything He would ever do. Joseph's silent strength was what kept his family grounded.

HE WAS HIS FAMILY'S PROTECTOR

When King Herod heard about the birth of Jesus, he sought to kill Him, but Joseph had a dream being commissioned by God to take his little family to Egypt for safety, and that's exactly what he did. Not only that, even when Herod died and the angel appeared again to return to his native town, he still refused to go but instead settled at Nazareth due to fear of any impending danger. That is what a Joseph does—he goes beyond his way, anticipating anything that threatens the danger of his family. He wasn't going to take any chances and regret them later.

His intention of settling in Nazareth was for Jesus to be well covered and protected until the right time, when He would be revealed to the world. Any good husband and father would do just that—focus on his family safety first—because he understands that his primary role is to protect them.

I really honor and respect Joseph because he showed to us that sometimes, it is okay to be the engine behind the car and not necessarily be noticed as the driver. Yet, without you, the car will never move, which would mean that no one can actually drive the car. Needless to say, his role was equally crucial for the manifestation of the Son of God becoming man and fulfilling His purpose of destroying the works of the devil (1 John 3:8).

MODERN DAY JOSEPHS

A Joseph always provides stability and covering for their baby to be nurtured and guards it until they are birthed. They are fatherly figures and shepherds who watch over the day-to-day needs of not just you but also the baby you carry. I'd likened Joseph's role to that of a pastor.

Unlike Elizabeth, your Joseph will be more intimate with you. While you need an Elizabeth to coach you in the way you should go, you need a Joseph to be with you every step of the way until you give birth. He gets to see you endure daily pregnancy symptoms and he gets to cheer you on even though he doesn't understand what you are enduring, because his job is to provide presence and a listening ear to you as you undergo all the various changes happening to your body.

What makes "Josephs" silent heroes is the fact that they are not interested in being in the limelight. Rather, they are more interested in fulfilling their function, which is to take you in, love on you just the way you are, and cheer you on as you birth and raise your baby. Sometimes, they become the midwives of your baby as it was in the case of Mary. She was alone in the inn with Joseph and the animals. Their roles are permanent, while Elizabeths' roles are temporary. Elizabeths may see you pregnant and even witness the birth of your baby, but the role of Joseph is irreplaceable!

Therefore, in pursuit of your visions and dreams, you can have many Elizabeths. Sometimes, one vision would require many Elizabeths because, as each phase or season of your dream progresses, it would demand different people to come into your life, but a Joseph is always constant. "For though you might have ten thousand instructors in Christ, yet you do not have many fathers; for in Christ Jesus I have begotten you through the gospel" (1 Cor. 4:15 NKJV).

FINDING YOUR JOSEPH

Just like the process of handpicking Elizabeth, it is not your place to choose your Joseph. The Lord sovereignly chooses your Joseph for you, whether through direct divine visitation or providence.

He will also confirm with Joseph his responsibility in your life. Remember, when God spoke to Mary and she accepted the call to be the mother of Jesus, there was never a mention of Joseph in that discussion. In fact, the only human element mentioned in the scenario was Elizabeth, but when it came to Joseph, God spoke to him directly. You don't have to convince Joseph to cover you; if God appointed them, He would speak to them directly on your behalf!

So, how do you identify yours? Well, in Mary's case, it was her husband. Your Joseph may not be your spouse. They could be your parent, pastor, friend, business partner, or a mere stranger who comes into your life, sent by God to play that specific role. Sometimes too, your Elizabeth can also be your Joseph—God can use the same person to play the dual role in your life.
Never underestimate the Presence of a Joseph in your life!

The Prophetic Watchmen of Jesus: Simeon & Anna the Prophetess

Up until the baby Jesus was born, nobody knew that there were other people who were also "hidden in plain sight" but waiting to "see" the birth of Jesus, nonetheless. They were actively seeking God in prayer until the Savior was born. That was the résumé for Simeon the priest, and Anna the prophetess.

Little is known about them, but Luke chapter 2 tells briefly about the volume of the work they have been doing "behind the scenes" in the birthing Jesus. Luke relates that the Holy Spirit had revealed to Simeon, a just and devout man, that he would not die until he had seen the savior being born (Luke 2:26).

Anna, on the other hand, was a prophetess. Scripture narrates that she had been married for only seven years, and has been a widow for eighty-four years. The Bible says she never left the temple but served God with fasting and prayer night and day (Luke 2:36–37).

When the baby Jesus was brought to the temple in Jerusalem to be presented to the Lord as the firstborn son, according to the custom of the law, those two beheld Him, led by the Spirit, they were also at the temple that day. Simeon held the child in his hand and began to prophesy about His destiny: *"for my eyes have seen Your salvation which You have prepared before the face of all peoples, a light to bring revelation to the Gentiles, and the glory of your people Israel"* (Luke 2:30–32). Anna also beheld the baby Jesus and testified about Him to all who look for redemption in Jerusalem (Luke 2:38).

Prayer and intercession are very necessary for the birthing of your dreams. Just because God has spoken to you and you are all in action does not automatically guarantee its manifestation. This is because there are external forces that will try to hinder and even abort them if they have the chance. Therefore, you should inoculate your dreams and visions with prayers, and God provides prophetic intercessors to cover you so your prophetic destiny can be secured.

We need intercession because everything God has said about you, especially dreams that will have global impact, will always have contention in the spirit realm. Thus, without prayer, they will be aborted.

THE POWER OF PROPHETIC INTERCESSION

> "I have set watchmen on your walls, O Jerusalem; They shall never hold their peace day or night. You who make mention of the Lord, do not keep silent, And give Him no rest till He establishes And till He makes Jerusalem a praise in the earth."

(ISA. 62:6-7).

Almost every new move, big movement, and revival that has taken place happened because someone or a group of people prayed. John Wesley once said, "*God does nothing except in response to believing prayer.*"27

While the lifeblood of every Christian is prayer, there are people who have been appointed or set apart by the Holy Spirit and called into this responsibility of interceding. These people become watchmen, and they watch and pray, sometimes travailing for a period of time until the counsel of God is established or manifested concerning the people, nations, and the world at large.

A prophetic intercessor is, therefore, someone who is directly being influenced by God to intercede according to the direction of the Holy Spirit. They are gifted with the ability to pray and seek the face of God concerning His will. They may not be known in the public eye but have a major influence in the "Secret Place"—Heaven recognizes them as heroes.

JESUS, OUR GREATEST INTERCESSOR

Perhaps the best way to really understand the power of intercession is to study the role of the High Priest and his duty on the Day of Atonement in the tabernacle. In Exodus 25:8–9, and 40, Moses received a detailed and specific architectural blueprint to build a portable tent in which God would dwell amongst His people in the wilderness—the tabernacle. This was going to be the hub where the glory of God would be revealed, a replica of what is already in Heaven.

However, due to our spiritual death, we didn't have direct access to God, and we were unable to restore that relationship on our own. Although God is merciful, He is also a just God. Therefore, the wages of sin could not be forgiven without blood sacrifice as He said in His Word that the life of a person is in the blood. The only way to satisfy the injustice of sin is by the shedding of blood. Hence, the need for a high priest.

Much of the High Priest's activity on the Day of Atonement is listed in details in Leviticus 16, and I strongly suggest you read the entire passage to fully grasp the weight of this revelation. In summary, the High Priest would change from his priestly garments to white linen robes like the rest of Jewish people as a sign of repentance for sin. Then he would enter into the Holy of Holies, which was separated from the rest of the Holy Place by a thick curtain, a veil which served as a barrier between God and men. The High Priest could only cross this barrier after having first been cleansed from his sinfulness, and only on the annual Day of Atonement. Otherwise, he was a dead man.

Then he would enter into the Holy of Holies, which contained only one article of furnishing, the Ark of the Covenant. The High Priest would then sprinkle the blood of the bullock he sacrificed for his sins onto the floor before the Ark and onto the Mercy Seat, which was positioned on top.

The High Priest will go on further to cast lots over two live goats which were brought by the people. One would be slain as a sin offering for the nation. Its blood was sprinkled on the Mercy Seat of the Ark, which symbolized that the people's sins were covered.

The sins of the people were then confessed over the second goat, called the scapegoat, symbolically transferring their sins to it. This goat was released into the wilderness to symbolize the complete removal of their sins.

Once he completes these duties, the High Priest puts his priestly garments back on and made a burnt offering of both the bullock and the goat outside. And in the Old Testament days, this practice had to be performed annually to atone for the people's sins until Jesus came and died once and for all as the perfect sacrifice.

Now, the writer of Hebrews makes a direct correlation between Jesus being our High Priest and the Tabernacle. Just take a look at this passage from Hebrews:

"Since then we have a great high priest who has passed through the heavens, Jesus, the Son of God, let us hold fast our confession. For we do not have a high priest who is unable to sympathize with our weaknesses, but one who in every respect has been tempted as we are, yet without sin. Let us then with confidence draw near to the throne of grace, that we may receive mercy and find grace to help in time of need. For every high priest chosen from among men is appointed to act on behalf of men in relation to God, to offer gifts and sacrifices for sins. He can deal gently with the ignorant and wayward, since he himself is beset with weakness. Because of this he is obligated to offer sacrifice for his own sins just as he does for those of the people. And no one takes this honor for himself, but only when called by God, just as Aaron was. So also Christ did exalt himself to be made high priest but was appointed by him who said to him, "You are my Son, today I have begotten you;" as he says also in another place, "You are a priest forever, after the order of Melchizedek." In the days of his flesh, Jesus offered up prayers and supplications, with loud cries and tears, to him who was able to save him from death, and he was heard because of his reverence. Although he was a son, he learned obedience through what he suffered. And being made perfect, he became the source of eternal salvation to all who obey him, being designated by God a high priest after the order of Melchizedek"

(HEB. 4:14; 5:10)

As you can see from the above scriptures, the ultimate role of the

High Priest in the tabernacle was to act on behalf of men in relation to God and to offer gifts and sacrifices for sins. Simply put, his role was to intercede on behalf of the people to God. Therefore, Jesus Christ performs the office of the High Priest by becoming the perfect sacrifice to satisfy the injustice of sin, to reconcile us to God, and is currently making continual intercession for us before God.

Hence, the greatest act of Jesus's love for us today is that He is busily in Heaven, pleading your case before the Father, asking God to shower down His blessings on you regardless of your struggles. Intercession starts from the throne room in heaven, which also serves as the court house of heaven where divine counsel and judgment are always being dispensed, and Jesus our Redeemer, is right there, pleading on our behalf through His blood.

THE HOLY SPIRIT INTERCEDES ON OUR BEHALF

To make our lives even more wonderful, the third person of the Trinity also intercedes for us. The Book of Romans assures us that the Holy Spirit helps us in our weakness and prays for us with wordless groans because we don't know what we ought to pray, and He prays according to the will of God for us (Rom. 8:26–27).

This shows the level of relevance that Heaven puts on Intercession. Hence, the greatest calling on a believer's life is the call to intercession. Without intercessors, nothing gets done on earth because intercessors or God's watchmen, stand at their posts to enforce Heaven's decree on earth through prayer. Sometimes, they may even negotiate on God's behalf and act as a mediator concerning revelations that have been revealed to them. They may receive a burden or an urge to pray or receive insight from God through prophetic revelation such as a Scripture, vision, or word, or a feeling.

PROPHETIC INTERCESSION PAVES WAY FOR THE BIRTHING OF PROPHETIC PROMISE!

If Jesus needed a human prophetic intercessor or watchman to pray for Him, then you also need watchmen. One woman of God lived in the temple, praying night and day to ensure that His manifestation and the fulfillment of His calling was going to come to fruition. In other words, God made sure that He secured the destiny of Jesus with prayer to guarantee success.

Thus, Prophetic Intercession can signify a security deposit, a transaction in the spirit realm that guarantees that your prophetic destiny is established.

This is why it is essential to dream with God; He employs people to stand in the gap for you and reinforce His will for your life so that nothing hinders you. God has someone praying for you!

As you are reading this, you may be called into the ministry of the intercessor. I want to encourage you to never stop praying, because your prayers are working. The people on whose behalf you are praying may never know you, but your impact in their lives through prayer is more effective than any strategy they will set up for themselves.

Anna the prophetess stayed in the temple day and night, praying and interceding until the Savior was announced. Every vision from God that will impact the world and many generations would require an "Anna" to be the watchman. We need prophetic intercessors who bombard heaven 24/7, praying down the counsel of God on earth as it is in heaven.

KEY TAKEAWAY: You need a parent, pastor, and intercessor to actualize your dreams and sustain them. We call them your silent heroes. They may not be in the limelight with you but their impact on your destiny can never be erased.

10

Embracing Your Tribe

Have you ever been to any major sporting event at a stadium? if you have you must have encountered a group of people dressed in cute little jerseys, wearing sneakers with happy faces, shouting, and doing all sorts of choreography to entertain the crowd and encourage them to join them in cheering their favorite team on. We call them cheerleaders.

Cheerleading is an activity in which the participants (the cheerleaders) cheer for their team as a form of encouragement or lead the fans among the spectators to cheer their favorite team to keep them going until they win the game. A cheerleader shows complete faith in the players; they are their number one fans, and they do a lot of creative things to motivate the team so they can keep up the team's spirit. Their ultimate purpose is to see their favorite team win the game, and they are there to help you do just that!

In the game of life, there are a bunch of people that need to cheer you on as you pursue your God-given mandate. I call them your cheerers. These are the people ordained by God to be the first to believe in you and celebrate you before the rest of the world catches up on you and supports your vision with substance. Even after the world finds you out, your cheerers will keep you on your course.

Jesus had His own cheerers at His birth: the angels, the shepherds, and the Wise Men from the East!

Heaven's Publicity

The angels of God were celebrating Jesus before anyone found about Him:

> "And suddenly there was with the angel a multitude of the heavenly hosts praising God and saying: Glory to God in the Highest, and on earth peace, goodwill toward men!"
>
> (LUKE 2:14).

This was the experience a group of shepherds witnessed one glorious night. They had received a message from one angel about the birth of a savior, and suddenly, a band of angels surrounded the one angel, and they all began to celebrate; in other words, cheer on about the birth of Jesus to the world.

When you embrace the calling of your life, heaven immediately begins to celebrate you even when you don't feel it. Mary didn't know angels were singing and celebrating the birth of Jesus, yet Heaven was throwing a party: glory in the highest!

Anytime you say yes to God; heaven throws a party for partnering with God!

"Therefore we also, since we are surrounded by so great a cloud of witnesses, let us lay aside every weight, and the sin which so easily ensnares us, and let us run with endurance the race that is set before us, looking unto Jesus, the author and finisher of our faith"

(HEB. 12:1–2).

Heaven is cheering you on!

Earthly Resources

There was another group of people who celebrated the birth of Jesus. These were known in the Bible as the Wise Men from the East. They came to celebrate the birth of the king by paying homage, which also meant they worshipped Him with their substance. They came because they had seen His star from the East and had come to pay homage to Him.

Historical findings reveal that it was the custom of the ancient kings and the Magi of the Chaldeans, to consult signs of the Zodiac about all the affairs of their lives. Consulting the signs of the Zodiac was the study of the motions of the stars, and through their study they were able to know and understand life events before they happened. They would foretell weather to inform and also warn of impending danger such as a storm. The Magi would likely be referred to as astrologists in our modern world because they always studied the weather and the astral world.

Thus, they studied the star that appeared in the sky, which got them to do further investigation and they discovered that a mighty king was born.

You could be wondering why God would have allowed a star to appear in the sky for these wise men to see. The answer is very simple: Jesus was king, so God made sure that the king in Him was honored!

HOW DOES THIS APPLY TO YOU?

You need people who can celebrate your worth regardless of your imperfections. The wise men didn't come because Jesus had sat on the throne, after all, he was just a baby; yet, they came and bowed down. Not only that, they also presented gifts to Him because you don't visit a king without presenting him with gifts.

God will cause your greatness to be seen by people far away. Respected people and those of prominence who have the resources to help you actualize it will pay homage to your worth. These are the destiny financiers and helpers who have the connections and resources to help you. They may not even know you, but they have been mandated by God to support your "baby" materially and financially.

LIKE-MINDEDNESS

The shepherds got to hear about the news of Christ's birth through the angels, and they came to celebrate Jesus. Why shepherds? Because Jesus was the chief shepherd, so God made sure that He had that association celebrate His Son's birth on earth whose primary job was to shepherd our souls..

Now, you may be wondering how this applies to you? Well, it does apply in many ways. If you are going to be successful in fulfilling your God-given vision, you must never underestimate the power of the right associations. Because Jesus was the chief shepherd (1 Peter 5:4), God made sure He allowed His tribe to celebrate Him. If you know God is calling you in an area of expertise, you can't afford to neglect the gathering of those tribes around you because iron sharpens iron (Prov. 27:17).

THE POWER OF ASSOCIATION

"Your network is your net worth"

—PORTER GALE[28]

You can never underestimate the power of an association. Anytime a group of people gathers, whatever their cause, their unity and bond are a strong guarantee of success and exponential results whether their goal is positive or negative.

We were first introduced to the potential atomic power of association by the almighty Himself when He saw from Heaven that humanity was aiming for something bigger than themselves, and they tapped into the universal principle of oneness. Now, for Bible gurus, I know we have all read the story of the Tower of Babel, found in Genesis:

Now the whole earth had one language and one [a]speech. And it came to pass, as they journeyed from the east, that they found a plain in the land of Shinar, and they dwelt there. Then they said to one another, "Come, let us make bricks and [b]bake them thoroughly." They had brick for stone, and they had asphalt for mortar. And they said, "Come, let us build ourselves a city, and a tower whose top is in the heavens; let us make a name for ourselves, lest we be scattered abroad over the face of the whole earth." But the Lord came down to see the city and the tower which the sons of men had built. And the Lord said, "Indeed the people are one and they all have one language, and this is what they begin to do; now nothing that they propose to do will be withheld from them. Come, let Us go down and there confuse their language, that they may not understand one another's speech." So the Lord scattered them abroad from there over the face of all the earth, and they ceased building the city. Therefore its name is called [c]Babel, because there the Lord confused the language of all the earth; and from there the Lord scattered them abroad over the face of all the earth.

(GEN. 11:1–9)

This short passage in the Bible is so profoundly powerful because in it we discover that mankind has a very powerful weapon that is guaranteed to work every time we want to embark on any mission—find a gathering of like-minded people and join forces with them to make your dream a reality. We call these synergistic relationships.

In other words, when you are in a company of people, their energy and personality rub off on you and vice versa. This is why the Bible admonishes us to stay away from bad company, because they corrupt good character and do not make you effective in life (1 Cor. 15:33; Ps. 1:1). In the same token, we are encouraged to pursue healthy and positive relationships and the company of people who will help us become the best version of ourselves:

"Walk with the wise and you become wise." (Prov. 13:2)
"As iron sharpens iron, so a man sharpens the countenance of his friend." (Prov. 27:17)
"Where there is no counsel, the people fail; but in the multitude of counselors there is safety." (Prov. 11:14).

Relationships can either make or mar you. I'm sure all of us have seen the effects relationships have had on people, positively or negatively. Therefore, we have to be very mindful and intentional of who we choose to hang out with and those we allow to come into our circle because when you are starting out on any venture, the right relationships or endorsements from the right association can open doors for you in ways that you could not do on your own.

A great biblical example of this is the friendship between David and Jonathan according to 1 Samuel,

> "Now when he had finished speaking to Saul, the [a]soul of Jonathan was knit to the soul of David, and Jonathan loved him as his own soul. Saul took him that day, and would not let him go home to his father's house anymore. Then Jonathan and David made a covenant, because he loved him as his own soul"

(1 SAM. 18:1–3).

This healthy friendship will continue as chapter 19 revealed Saul's intention trying to get his son to betray and kill David. However, we saw him protect David and later on in life. David honored his friend by showing favor to his disabled son, Mephibosheth. According to 2 Samuel 9, when David was looking to bless Saul's house, he learned about the tragedy of Mephibosheth and decided to give him his father Jonathan inheritance, in addition to eating from the royal table permanently.

This really paints a picture of the potential of the type of healthy relationship that God wants us to have. Whether through friendship, marriage, or any other healthy relationship, it must be beneficial to both parties and bring glory to God. In contrast, the wrong relationship can mess up your life, goals, and plans more than you could ever imagine. Many of us have aborted awesome visions and dreams from God because we spoke with the wrong people, and they discouraged us. Therefore, we couldn't proceed and progress.

I am here to charge you to start investing in the right relationships for your life and dreams. Start investing time and your presence in people and associations that will improve your life and also find ways you too can positively enhance others as well. Anything dysfunctional or toxic, make a decision to cut yourself from those ties—be they personal, romantic, or professional relationships.

Now, in today's world, there are many ways to plug into a healthy and thriving community:
—Join a physical gathering such as a church, fellowship, club, or professional association that is heading towards the same direction of your dreams.
—Secondly, you can plug into virtual associations. Social media has made the world a global village. Take advantage of these technological advancements and plug into social media groups and other on-

line communities that nourish you and empower you to thrive in your purpose and dreams.

Hanging around the right associations that are focused on your dreams and goals will help you grow exponentially; they are heading towards a similar destination and can offer you suggestions, recommendations, and also tools on how to reach your goals. What a better way to get an endorsement from any of them, especially when you are starting out!

You can even get an internship, volunteer, and even job opportunities just by speaking with the right people. You need this association to cheer you on. Sometimes, they are the only squad you have until the rest of the world catches up.

Isn't this amazing? That just one simple yes from Mary to give birth to Jesus brought forth all these amazing people. You don't have to toil and struggle your way through the vision God has given you. You only need to respond to Him, and He will align everything and everyone on your path to make it happen.

Your Assigned Audience

For every assignment, there is an assigned audience. You must realize that everyone is not your audience. However, if God gave you a commission, rest assured that there are a group of people who would need the solution(s) you have been created to solve. This is what I have coined as your dream receptors. Another common term used in the corporate world is your "Tribe."

The reason I used the term "receptors" is because in the field of biology, a receptor can simply be defined as a cell that receives signals and initiates response.[29]

In 1 Samuel, when the young David was restless, hiding away from King Saul, something began to happen that would position him to the leader that God has called him:

> "David therefore departed from there and escaped to the cave of Adullam. So when his brothers and all his father's house heard it, they went down there to him. And everyone who was in distress, everyone who was in debt, and everyone who was [a]discontented gathered to him. So he became captain over them. And there were about four hundred men with him"

(1 SAM.22:1–2 NKJV).

Just like David, you will not succeed everywhere. However, your dream receptors will value your time, gifts, talents, services, and anointing because what you have been given is for them.

Just like David, as you step out in the assigned tasks, these people will follow suit as long as you stay consistent on your assignment(s). They will end up being your greatest supporters; those who will mostly finance your visions and make a major buzz about you because of the impact you've had on them, and they will also be the ones who will continue your legacy even after you're gone from this planet.

Therefore, determine in your heart to give yourself solely for the betterment of your dream receptors because it will pay off the biggest.

KEY TAKEAWAY: When you step out to realize your dreams and visions, God will bring a community to you. Some will cheer you and push you, and others will be the ones who will drink from your well. You need them both to fulfill your mandate.

small acts change the world

SECTION III

Unpacking #YourSuccessHacks

Do you know that there are principles set by God to help you to not only realize your dreams but also help you enjoy long-term good success in everything. It's one thing to start something and it is another to finish. We want to reach the finish line don't we? Well, girlfriend, in this section, you will be discovering one of the ancient keys that will give you access to unlimited results. This is guaranteed to help you succeed every time.

11

The Secret to Long Term Success

"... He leads me in the paths of righteousness For His name's sake"

(PS. 23:3)

God created and planned for us to excel in our life mandates. In executing this goal, He set life principles and laws in motion to aid us. Therefore, as long as we follow the principles set in place, we are guaranteed to succeed because we have been wired to excel in our life mandate. As a matter of fact, He stamped His integrity at the expense of our success because He wants to assure us that the mandate is very important to Him and He wants the best for us.

There are two principles:
1. Honoring the relationships God has given you
2. Honoring the laws and principles that God has set in place

Every promise in God's word that is guaranteed to bless us operates mainly in these two principles; either you obey the instructions and respect the process of life or value the relationships He brings, because God works through people.

The Law of Honor

What and who you honor multiplies in your life and serves you well and what and who you dishonor exits out of your life.

In the Book of Exodus, when God was giving the law that the new Jewish nation was to follow, He specifically mentioned in the sixth commandment: *"Honor Your Father and Mother that your days may be long on earth"* (Ex. 20:12).

In other words, God was telling the Israelites that if you want to have a long life on earth, that depends on how well you honor your parents, if you dishonor them, even if you obey all the laws of the land, you will still die early.

This also makes me understand that the people who parent us have authority over us in ways that heaven bears witness to. And if you will learn how honor works, not just for our life longevity, but in everything else, including our goals and dreams, you are guaranteed to succeed.

So, what then is honor?

The Merriam-Webster dictionary defines *honor* (as a noun) as *"high respect, great esteem."*[30] As a verb, it is defined as *"adherence to what is right or to a conventional standard of conduct; to regard with great respect; to fulfill an obligation or keep an agreement; to regard or treat with admiration and respect; to give special recognition."*[31]

Therefore, to honor something or someone is to do the following aforementioned definitions.

1. The Secret to Longevity

> "He who receives you receives Me, and He who receives Me receives Him who sent me. He who receives a prophet in the name of a prophet shall receive a prophet's reward. And he who receives a righteous man in the name of a righteous man shall receive a righteous man's reward"
>
> (MATT. 10:41)

The above text is actually a quote by Jesus. This was when He was about to send the twelve disciples out to apply the mentorship lessons He has been teaching them. As He gave them the instructions, He mentioned this to let them understand the gravity of the authority He was entrusting in their care—that anyone who welcomed them has indirectly welcomed Jesus because they were going in His honor. Hence, they would receive the corresponding rewards for welcoming Jesus through His disciples.

Then Jesus received a key secret through those words: if you receive a prophet in the office of the prophet, you will receive a reward that comes with a prophet. The same applied to a righteous man. In other words, there are different rewards for different offices. And if you receive the person who stands in that office, the corresponding reward reserved for that office comes to you. What a profound revelation! Therefore, it really didn't matter if Jesus was your biological son like Mary and Joseph or brother like He was to John and James. As long as they saw Jesus as their earthly brother, they would never get the Son of God's reward, but if they saw Him as God, then they would receive the reward in that office of the Son of God.

This makes me understand that your progress in life is determined by what and who you honor. There are some things in life you don't have to pray into success. Honor will produce things your longest hour(s) of prayer or handwork can never produce. Even Jesus could not perform healing and miracles in some places because they failed to honor Him and recognize Him as the Messiah. Therefore, although Emmanuel walked amongst them, their dishonor blinded them from tapping into divine visitation. As long as they saw Him as the carpenter's son, they only received the carpenter's outcome. Those who valued Jesus as the Son of God, the promised Messiah, also encountered divinity.

A typical example of this was the woman with the issue of blood. She put so much value and expectation on the healing power of Jesus. Therefore, regardless of the crowd, she only touched the hem of His garment, and virtue immediately left Jesus because she respected Jesus as the healer and even didn't need Him to touch her physically.

Familiar is the killer of blessings. What you've deemed as common will always produce common results in your life. If you don't value a person or a thing in your life, you will never enjoy them, and that blessing will leave.

Every law is based on the principle of honor. For instance, if you respect the laws of God and you follow them accordingly, you will prosper, but if you disobey, there are consequences. Another example is in the country and the place where you currently dwell. If you obey the laws of the land, you'll walk happy and free, but if you break the rules, you'll face the consequential discipline.

I know the same principles follow us at work and all institutions. Obey the law and you remain there; disrespect the law and you are bound to be fired or dropped out.

Likewise, every possibility that we will need in life has already been provided by our Heavenly Father (2 Peter 1:3), but many of them are locked inside the realm of honor. If we will master this powerful principle, longevity and good success will always be guaranteed.

My question to you today is, what laws have you dishonored that has caused you to suffer in life? Which person or people have you despised in your heart that has caused heaven to be closed on you in that area?

Here are some ways to show value and honor the people that God has placed in your life.

HONOR THE PRESENCE OF THE HOLY SPIRIT IN YOUR LIFE.

> "[I]n all your ways, ACKNOWLEDGE HIM and He will direct your path"
>
> (PROV. 3:6 EMPHASIS ADDED).

The Holy Spirit's abiding Presence in your life is Jesus Gift to you to comfort, direct and empower you for your mandate. He is a gift that we are not to take for granted. When you recognize His Presence and Lordship in your life, you will always prosper.

PRAY FOR THE PEOPLE IN YOUR LIFE DAILY AND SOMETIMES PRAY WITH THEM.

They are not only being bombarded with menial tasks and life struggles but pray that they persevere through everything. Also, pray for their families, health, wellbeing, and finances.

Sometimes too, pray with them. Let them see you bear their burdens as they bear the burden of the responsibility of caring for you and nurturing your vision.

INVEST IN THEIR LIVES AND DREAMS TOO

Don't be too selfish or so caught up in seeing your vision and dream born that you fail to see what your squad is also doing in their own lives. Show interest by finding out what they are currently doing and serve them. Invest time and resources, including money, so they can happily serve you. Jesus was known as the carpenter's son because his father was a carpenter! He served his father's business.

OFFER WORDS OF ENCOURAGEMENT.

> "A word fitly spoken are apples of God on a slate of silver"
>
> (PROV. 25:11–13).

Be seasonal with your words. Be sensitive to their needs. Know when to speak life and when not to speak. Sometimes, the best gift you can give to others is your gift of presence. Not saying anything at all can sometimes be all that is needed.

RESPECT THEIR LEADERSHIP OVER YOU BY SUBMITTING TO THEM.

You may be the most favored one, but you need them to make it; therefore, make sure you respect and also listen to instructions, corrections, and counsel given by them. If they are vouching for you, then you want some of them in your inner circle to align you when you miss it sometimes.

SHOW UP FOR THEM.

Don't be available only when you need something. Make yourself present in their lives as well and take a lot of initiatives to keep them around you. People who value and love you and believe in you are hard to come by. Some of them may even annoy you or hurt your feelings sometimes, or you may not like the way they discipline you. However, let them know you value them through your actions. Jesus, although He was the Son of God, became a carpenter by trade because His earthly father was a carpenter. Sometimes, it is okay to put your accolades and titles down, so that you can celebrate a brother or sister who is being a blessing to you. By showing up for them, you increase the longevity of your greatness because the Lord always rewards people who honor others, especially those who serve as fatherly and motherly figures in our lives.

COVER THEIR NAKEDNESS

Just as they are providing refuge, moral support, and covering in the pursuit of your dreams and assignments, you must cover their shortcomings, weaknesses, and flaws. Remember the story of Noah and his sons? The Bible relates that after the flood one night, their father, Noah, got drunk and one of his sons, bumped into his father's nakedness and came out telling his brothers publicly. The remaining two, however, did the opposite. The Bible says they took clothes and entered into the room backward and covered their father's nakedness.

Interestingly enough, when Noah woke up, he knew what his son had done, and he cursed him. Be very careful about how you treat those who have invested in you. It may not be much and always make sure that you give the due respect when needed and let God fight your battles even when they wrong you. Although Noah was wrong to be drunk, it was not his son's place to even see his father's nakedness let alone make noise about it. Sometimes, God gives us a peek into our elders' nakedness so we can cover them.

2. *The Secret to Good Success*

> "This Book of the Law shall not depart from your mouth, but you shall meditate in it day and night, that you may observe to do according to all that is written in it. For then you will make your way (your dreams and visions) prosperous, and then you will have good success."
>
> (JOSHUA 1:8, EMPHASIS ADDED)

HONOR GOD'S WORD AND YOU WILL PROSPER (PROV. 4:20).

The first time success was ever mentioned in the Bible was by God Himself when He was encouraging Joshua to take the baton passed down to him by his mentor, Moses. Through this scripture, we discover that the secret to good success in God is always hidden in His Word, and if we diligently follow all the precepts written in it, we are guaranteeing our "way" prosperous and we have good success.

In other words, if you and I are responsible for guaranteeing good success, which also proves that there is bad success, when you don't follow the instructions in God's Word, you are guaranteeing failure and bad success. If you put other people's opinions, philosophies, and religious belief systems as your guiding posts, well Girl, that is recipe for disaster. You may start well, but you will end up in a big mess because nothing lasts if it is not from God. God's Word and principles are the only guaranteed tools to make you succeed the good way without any troubles and repercussions.

Listed below are a few principles that are guaranteed to help you on your path of good success as you pursue your God-given dreams:

HONOR TIME (ECCL. 12:1; EPH. 5:15–16).

Time is the richest gift you ever received from God to help you fulfill your mandate. This is because almost everything can be bought but time, once lost time can never be retrieved unless God redeems the time for you. This makes it a very important component when going after your goals and dreams. Mary, right after the angel spoke to her, responded quickly. The Bible says she rose up and hurriedly visited her cousin Elizabeth (Luke 1:39). When God gives you a vision or dream, start right away. Don't waste time. Invest time wisely, and maximize it to your advantage in the days of your youth so you can have more accomplished now as you build your life.

CAPITALIZE ON OPPORTUNITIES (ECCL. 12:1).

Dreams and visions are realized when we capitalize on opportunities presented to us. This is because dreams and visions are progressive. You don't become everything in a day, but you build upon what you start today. Opportunities, or what the Bible coins "chance," are given a period of time wrapped in circumstances but are promised to every human being. Everything you will ever become will, more often than not, present itself in opportunities, and when you take advantage of them, you will progress in your goal. The problem is that most of us don't recognize them because they usually come camouflaged in problems, and we tend to focus on the negative that we didn't realize that the situation was meant to help us realize our dreams and visions faster.

God guaranteed that we will be given chances. Whether you will get more than one is subjective, but He did promise all of us will at least have one. If we will be honest with ourselves, we've all been given numerous chances but blew them. Ask yourself today: what are you doing with the given moments and chances you have been given? If you are in a difficult situation right now, ask yourself: What is this teaching me? How do I maximize this to realize my dreams? What character or skills am I developing from it? All of these factors will help you to take advantage of the chances that are currently around you. Start seeing things through the lens of your dreams and visions. Maybe what you consider an obstacle to your goals may actually become a catalyst to help materialize them faster.

USE WHAT YOU'VE BEEN GIVEN.

In Exodus chapter 4, when God was commissioning Moses to deliver His oppressed people from Egypt, Moses began to list all the excuses possible to disqualify him from the mandate. But God told him to look into his hand, it was there Moses realized that his forty-year shepherd experience were actually not in vain. God was using this experience to hone Moses's skills as a shepherd for his people and this applies to you, too. What do you have in your hand? What talents, skills, experience of life, and gifts have you been given by God? This is what God will use to help you accomplish the tasks He has for you. Therefore, don't despise them no matter how insignificant or undignified they look now.

TAKE THE FIRST STEP.

> "So it came to pass, when Joseph had come to his brothers, that they stripped Joseph of his tunic, the tunic of many colors that was on him"
>
> (PS. 37:23).

To be *ordered* according to the dictionary is *"to give an authoritative direction or instruction to do something."*[32] The term is usually used in a courtroom when a judge commands the authority vested in them by the Government to issue a decree or pronounce a legal sentence or issue a verdict concerning a case.

Therefore, to have your steps ordered means your steps have been instructed or directed, which means your path is already pre-planned. In other words, there is nothing accidental about your path and the decisions you have to make in relation to your desires, goals, and dreams in life that God already doesn't know. In fact, He has already anticipated the outcome and made the necessary provisions and arrangements and contingency plans for them. Most of our outcomes will end up being discovery because God wants you to trust Him every step of the way, knowing that He is with you. So, go ahead and step out with all your fears, doubts, and surrender.

EMBRACE YOUR WEAKNESSES AND BE OPENED FOR CORRECTIONS.

The Bible has examples of people whose weakness got them

to face certain challenges that could have been prevented, making them go through a painful and longer route to fulfill their mandate. One prime example is Joseph. At a young age, God gave him a dream about his destiny and his big mouth got his jealous brother to sell him into slavery. Now God could have still gotten him into the place of prominence without going through hostility and pain, but he should have kept his mouth shut. Many of us go through unnecessary challenges and trials due to us not surrendering our weaknesses to the subjection of the Holy Spirit.

Certainly, His grace is sufficient to overcome any weakness, but until you yield to Him, you will still keep struggling. This is the time to do an inventory of your life, wherever you are struggling. Surrender to His leading and watch Him replace your weaknesses with His strength.

RESPECT THE LAWS OF NATURE AND PRINCIPLES OF THE LAND THAT GOD HAS SETTLED YOU.

In Mark, Jesus makes a very profound statement: "Render to Caesar the things that are Caesar's, and to God the things that are God's" (Mark 12:17). This was his response to the Pharisees for paying his tax to Caesar. Which means that Jesus respected the laws of the land that He dwelled. Likewise, we are to submit to the authorities that we have been put under and must respect the laws of the land and also in nature so we can stay out of trouble. Pay your taxes, obey the laws of your country, state and city. Make sure you keep things in proper balance and watch you soar into your greatness.

KEY TAKEAWAY : God wired you to succeed in your dreams and visions. He has set principles of honor in place to help you do just that. As long as you abide by them, you are guaranteed good success and longevity in your mandate.

Life is tough ···but··· so are YOU

SECTION IV

Unmasking #YourAdversary

Did you know there is an assassin after your mandate? This is the section you learn about him and his team who are working tirelessly against your progress in life. You will be exposed to everything fighting against you and also discover the mighty weapons you have at your disposal. Get ready to fight because you are at war. Let's conquer!

12

The Assassin Of Your Dreams

"The thief only comes to steal, kill, and destroy…"

(JOHN 10:10 WEB).

Just because your dreams and visions are from God doesn't mean you will not face opposition. Actually, most of your battles will stem from your decisions to realize them.

Here is a typical example:

> Now when they saw him afar off, even before he came near them, they conspired against him to kill him. Then they said to one another, "Look, this dreamer is coming! Come therefore, let us now kill him and cast him into some pit; and we shall say, "Some wild beast has devoured him." We shall see what will become of his dreams!

(GEN. 37:18–20 NKJV)

Everyone familiar with the Bible definitely knows about Joseph, and we can't talk about fulfilling your God-given dreams without bringing up one of the main Bible characters whose life is an actual example that God can bring your dreams and visions to pass no matter the obstacles you face.

We were first introduced to him in Genesis 37, as being the eleventh of twelve sons and loved more by his father, Jacob, than any of his other sons, because he was born to him in his old age by his beloved late wife, Rachel (Gen. 37:3).

To make matters worse, Joseph's father gifted him a coat of many colors, which was beautiful to behold but also ignited more envy from his brothers who were being starved of attention and love from the father. You can imagine the dilemma of Joseph and the dynamics of his relationship with his family. However, none propelled his brothers to kill him more than his big dream that he told them, not once but twice. His dreams got him potential murderers from his brothers who could no longer stand him.

The problem was not Joseph's dreams because God was the source, revealing His plans to him. The problem was telling the very people he knew were jealous of him. His big mouth almost cost him his life had God not intervened. I'm sure, he acted out of pure innocence but it cost him big time.

You must realize that that the enemy was not his brothers. There was someone working behind the scenes, capitalizing on the weaknesses of his brothers to slay him. This enemy didn't have a problem with Joseph the person but with his dream, because his dream, should it be realized would be one step further to the manifestation of the promise given to Abraham which was to eventually bring forth the Savior, Jesus.

Anytime, a dream or vision is given by God, there will be an opposition to see them fulfilled. To assume that you can accomplish anything from God and not encounter any challenge or resistance is an understatement. Just like Joseph, you also have an enemy! He never liked you and will forever hate you. If it's of God, be prepared to fight because you will face opposition.

> "Be on your guard and stay awake. Your enemy, the devil, is like a roaring lion, sneaking around to find someone to attack"
>
> (1 PETER 5:8 CEV).

Understand that you only have one enemy—the devil (Satan), but he is always hidden in plain sight and working within people (as we saw in Joseph's brothers). He saw an opportunity, an opened door through their jealousy to get rid of Joseph. Satan is always looking for ways and means to stop you from pursuing the assignment that God has given you, and he can use the people around us to abort them. What he fails to realize is that God has always gone ahead of him and drafted a masterplan to victory. Just as God intervened in Joseph's situation, God has an escape route to get you to your destiny.

So, who is this villain? Why is he so much after you and hates you so much? Well, God's Word reveals everything. Let's dive in.

In this section, we shall blow the whistle and uncover all the enemies against our progress and those in disguise. All of whom are working tirelessly to stop us from fulfilling our destiny. You will also be exposed to all the things fighting against you. More importantly, you will discover the mighty weapons you have at your disposal, which must be engaged for your desired and unending victory.

The Origin of Satan

The person or being known today as Satan, the adversary of the Christian, wasn't always the "Prince of Evil." It would surprise you to learn that someone who represents all that evil was once associated with so much good. Satan didn't emerge from the flames of hell, my friend. His story can be likened to that of fairy tales where beautiful princesses transform into ogres.

He wasn't always Satan. Initially, he was *Lucifer*, meaning "son of the morning," one of God's perfect creations. In Isaiah 42:12, God addresses Satan after his fall and says to him, "how art thou cut down to the ground."

However, in Ezekiel, chapter 28. the name Satan or Lucifer wasn't mentioned. Instead, we see *"the King of Tyrus"* and *"the anointed cherub,"* yet from the context and words used, we can easily discern that the passage also refers to our adversary, Satan, who isn't human but an angelic being.

For example, the same words used in Isaiah to describe Satan's fall are still used in Ezekiel chapter 28. And verse 17 says, *"Thine heart was lifted up because of thy beauty, thou hast corrupted thy wisdom by reason of thy brightness: I will cast thee to the ground...,"* which refers to his fall due to his sin.

Satan was created by God, full of wisdom and beauty, and the epitome of perfection. He was perfect in all his ways until sin was found in him. He was the anointed cherub, one of God's angels. In the Bible, cherubim are associated with the worship of God, His throne, and His glory.

Also, in Genesis, when Adam and Eve were sent out of Eden, it was cherubim who guarded the garden and the tree of life. All through scripture no other being or angel is referred to as the anointed cherub. This implies that Lucifer had a special place in God's service.

Furthermore, the Bible reveals that Lucifer had *tabrets* "timbrels or tambourines" and pipes attached to his form: *"the workmanship of thy tabrets and of thy pipes was prepared in thee in the day that thou was created"* (Ezek. 28:13). This gives us the idea that Satan indeed had something to do with music. So, Satan was formerly one of God's special angels and occupied a special place in heaven.

His Former Position

The Bible reveals that Satan formerly held the position of the anointed cherub, one of God's highest angels. Also, Satan was once in Eden, the garden of God. He was formerly called Lucifer which means son of the morning. Indeed, Lucifer was a creature of glory; he was covered with every precious stone, which can account for his name.

Ezekiel 28:17 says that Satan had corrupted his wisdom because of his "brightness." Such a being would have been a sight to behold. The way God lavished wisdom, beauty, and perfection on him imply that he was loved and favored by God. Verse 14 reveals that Lucifer before his fall was not only in Eden but also on the holy mountain of God. All over the Bible, the garden of Eden and God's holy mountain are used to depict God's presence. This adds up with the fact that Lucifer was a cherub. Cherubs are angelic beings whose position is in God's presence.

It is believed that, although Satan was the anointed cherub and dwelled in the mountain of God, he wasn't necessarily in heaven. For example, we saw that Satan was once in Eden, which is an earthly location.

Furthermore, Isaiah 14 reveals to us that Satan desired to ascend into heaven, above the heights of the clouds, and exalt his throne above the stars of God. This shows that Satan wasn't in heaven, he was under the clouds and beneath the stars. Also, it shows that he had a throne. Some biblical scholars believe that Satan had an earthly kingdom and indeed, Ezekiel 28 refers to him as the King of Tyrus, the power behind the Prince of Tyrus. Following the context, it was at this period that iniquity was found in him.

His Fall (Results of Satan's Sin)

"How art thou fallen from heaven, O Lucifer, son of the morning! How art thou cut down to the ground, which didst weaken the nations!"

(ISA. 14:12).

The scripture above can be misinterpreted to mean that Satan fell from heaven. But this was a revelation God gave to Isaiah concerning what would happen to Satan when he was judged and Jesus had been glorified. Because Isaiah 14:15–16 says, "*Yet thou shalt be brought down to hell, to the sides of the pit. They that see thee shall narrowly look upon thee, and consider thee, saying, Is this the man that made the earth to tremble, that did shake kingdoms?*"

Evidently, this is not a reference to the past but to the future, because Satan has not yet been judged and shamefully displayed before all the nations. And in Matthew 25:41, Jesus revealed in a parable of the kingdom that hell, which He called everlasting fire, is prepared for Satan and his angels. All these things put Isaiah 14:12 in a clearer perspective.

So, what was Satan's sin? Ezekiel 28:15 and 17 says that iniquity was found within him, and his heart was lifted up. Isaiah 14:13–14 reveals in more detail that Satan's sin was that of rebellion. He said in his heart that he will ascend into heaven and exalt his throne above the stars of God. He desired to sit on the mountain of the congregation (heaven's host); he wanted to take the place of God.

This was his sin. He coveted the worship and reverence that God received from all his creations. Satan, instead of seeing his privileged position amongst the angels as a reason to be humble, loyal, and faithful, saw it as an opportunity to be equal with God. This made God cast him out of His presence and pronounce judgment on him.

Ezekiel 28 says, "*by the multitude of thy merchandise they have filled the midst of thee with violence, and thou hast sinned: therefore, I will cast thee as profane out of the mountain of God: and will destroy thee, O covering cherub, from the midst of the stones of fire*" (Ezek. 28:16).

It is important to note that Satan's fall didn't only affect his position but also his nature. He was once the epitome of beauty and a light bearer but he becomes the master of darkness and evil. Satan has a great hatred for mankind, and this is because we occupy the position he coveted.

Man is created in God's image and likeness, and according to Ephesians 2:6, we are seated together with Christ who is seated on God's throne. As a result, Satan is all out to destroy man and make sure that he robs mankind of God's inheritance. His first attempt to do this was in the garden of Eden with Adam and Eve. Satan's deception in the garden led to the fall of man. Obviously, the devil wants man to be estranged from God's presence and doomed to everlasting fire just like himself.

His Present Location

The Bible portrays the devil as man's greatest enemy. Both the old and new testament reveal that evil and sin originated from Satan, who is always trying to make sure that man is unable to fulfill his God-given purpose. But it was the New Testament that he was referred to as our *adversary* which means "opponent." 1 Peter 5:8 says, *"your adversary the devil...."* He is our arch enemy. No wonder the Bible rightly calls him *"the accuser of the brethren"* (Rev. 12:10).

Understanding that Satan is our adversary is important to discerning his location. Believers have been described in God's word as soldiers. Yes, we are at war, and the opponent is Satan and his angels. Ephesians 6:12 talks about this war thus, *"for we wrestle not against flesh and blood but against principalities, against powers, against the rulers of the darkness of this world, against spiritual wickedness in high places."* It is believed that the highest rank in this classification of enemies is the fourth one—spiritual wickedness in high places—and the devil occupies this position with other wicked angels of his rank. In fact, some versions of the Bible say, "*in heavenly places.*"

It is believed that there are three heavens. Apostle Paul in 2 Corinthians 12:2 makes mention of being caught in the third heaven. Which I believe is where God dwells. Also, there are the atmospheric heavens where we fly our planes, which can be seen clearly from the earth. But it is believed that way beyond that is the second heaven where Satan dwells. This accounts for the fourth rank of demonic forces that live in high places.

Furthermore, Ephesians 2:2 calls Satan "*the prince of the power of the air.*" This means that Satan is in control of all the demonic forces that dwell in the second heaven. His power is in the "air."

ON EARTH

Also, Job 1 says, "*And the LORD said unto Satan, Whence comest thou? Then Satan answered the LORD, and said, From going to and fro in THE EARTH, and from walking up and down in it*" (Job 1:7, emphasis added). And 1 Peter 5:8 says he is like a lion walking about. Satan is a spirit, and we can deduce from this verse that he is currently active even on the earth.

Therefore, we can say that Satan is not really restricted to one location, and because he is not yet bound and tamed in a place, his activities on the earth are evident. Would you like to find out? Let's continue!

Satan's Activities against Christians

I believe you now know that Satan is your primary and only enemy. From the beginning, after the fall of man, God cursed the devil and created enmity between him and the seed of man. That includes you. So, the devil is all out contending with the children of God. He has succeeded in turning the earth into a war zone.

All he does is go about seeking his next victim. Who is the vulnerable person that he can bring down? Whose dream is the next precious one that he can frustrate and even abort? You also may be asking yourself, where is he? Where is his address so I can send a missile to destroy him once and for all? I wish it were that simple. I wish we could just locate him and then sentence him to jail that we may live peacefully and fulfill our dreams. Why did I say so?

UNMASKING THE DEVIL

> "And no wonder, for even Satan masquerades as an angel of light"
>
> (2 COR. 11:14 WEB).

Let me tell you the story of the first couple on earth. They were created in the likeness and image of God. They had absolute authority and dominion over all other creations. They ruled and reigned in a special garden called Eden, a place that plays host to God regularly to check on His privileged humans. What an awesome experience; life was fun, peaceful, and all things were in order. God also gave them a mandate, which is that other humans will proceed from them. They had one instruction in the garden: they must never eat of a particular tree located at the center of the garden.

One day, the devil came and a discussion ensued with Eve, the only woman on earth. He encouraged her to take a fruit from the tree they were commanded not to. He assured her that she was going to be like God (meanwhile, she was already created in God's image). He came in like somebody that has her interest at heart. He spoke softly, nicely, and convincingly so the woman couldn't help but eat of the fruit and gave it her husband. Eating the fruit was disobedience to God, and that led to their exit from Eden.

How come she didn't know it was the devil she was talking with? How come she could not decode that his intention was to separate them from the luxury of Eden? Why didn't she know that he was out to corrupt her seed? Have you found yourself asking any of these questions?

MASTER OF DISGUISE

For most people, Satan is portrayed as an ugly, dirty, shapeless, and unattractive figure with horns. If that was the case, don't you think it will be easy to just spot him and round him off? But really, most times he disguises himself. Clothed in beauty, he appears gentle and innocent like a sheep. He comes to our life to offer help and solutions to the very problem he started. He makes us laugh at sin and surrounds us with teachers that help to anesthetize the pain of sin and guilt.

This is why he is called "The Master of Disguise."

You know that a disguise makes one appear as something or someone other than who he really is. Did you see that scripture above? Paul sounded a note of warning to Christians that the devil can mask himself and disguise as an angel of light when he is actually an angel of darkness.

The activities of the devil against believers are not as we usually presume. No wonder the Bible says, "*so that we may not be outsmarted by Satan. After all, we are not unaware of his intentions*" (2 Cor. 2:11 ISV). This shows that there is a high tendency for Christians to be carried away and outsmarted by the devil. It's possible to play with the devil and not know till you are cut off from God and destroyed.

So, we need to know the devices of the devil, how he operates, so we can be better prepared against his activities and live the victorious life that Jesus has purchased for us.

What then are some of these activities?

He Tempts with Sin

He tried this with Jesus in Matthew 4 after He concluded a forty-day fast. He didn't succeed but he succeeded with Judas Iscariot. Friends, the devil is all out to separate you from God. Judas had a dream and vision of becoming an Apostle, but he lost it through the deception of the devil. Do you also want to see your dream fulfilled? Then flee from sin.

He Blindfolds Our Eyes from The Truth

> "I pray that God will open your minds to see his truth. … You will know that the blessings God has promised his holy people are rich and glorious"

(EPH. 1:18 ERV)

What you don't know, you cannot experience. Until you know what is available for you as a Christian, you may keep struggling in ignorance. So, the devil blinds the eyes of Christians from the blessings in redemption. Paul then prayed that our eyes be opened so we can see the promises of God and enjoy them.

He Does False Miracles

> "For false Christs and false prophets shall rise, and shall shew signs and wonders, to seduce, if it were possible, even the elect"

(MARK 13:22).

This was a statement by Jesus that the devil will use a lot of people to perform miracles and signs that are not from God but look real. Many people will be deceived and then follow such people and through that, they become trapped and unable to fulfill their dreams.

He Torments Christians

> "Ought not this woman, being a daughter of Abraham, whom Satan had bound eighteen long years, be freed from this bondage on the Sabbath day?"

(LUKE 13:16 WEB).

Jesus pointed out that Satan was behind the affliction of this woman for eighteen years. A lot of sicknesses today have no medical explanation or solution. They are simply the devil acting in the lives of people. (Although not all).

Demons

When Satan was cast down, he fell with some other angels who also rebelled against God:

> "And war broke out in heaven: Michael and his angels fought with the dragon; and the dragon and his angels fought, but they did not prevail, nor was a place found for hem in heaven any longer. So the great dragon was cast out, that serpent of old, called the Devil and Satan, who deceives the whole world; he was cast to the earth, and his angels were cast out with him."

(REV. 12:7–9).

These fallen angels became evil angels and the agents through whom he carries out his activities on the earth.

According to the Bible, the fallen angels have two categories:

1. Those who are actively working with the devil now.
2. Those who are currently bound in chains.

"For if God did not spare the angels who sinned, but cast them down to hell and delivered them into chains of darkness, to be reserved for judgment"

(2 PETER 2:4).

"And the angels who did not keep their [a]proper domain, but left their own abode, He has reserved in everlasting chains under darkness for the judgment of the great day"

(JUDE 6).

THE FIRST GROUP WORKING WITH THE DEVIL

"For we do not wrestle against flesh and blood, but against **principalities**, against **powers**, against the **rulers of the darkness of this age**, against **spiritual hosts of wickedness in the heavenly places**"

(EPH. 6:12, EMPHASIS ADDED).

Bible scholars believe that this chapter in Paul's Epistle to the Ephesian Church is written in military language of his time to depict a very serious spiritual reality to the believer. In this section, we will be doing a little grammar and research to the root words in order for us to comprehend the revelatory truths here. Because the New Testament was written in Greek, we are going to do a couple of word studies in Greek literature so you can actually understand how we landed on certain meanings.

The word *wrestle* is from the Greek word *palé*, and it means *"struggling, wrestling, or hand-to-hand fighting."*[33] Furthermore, *palé* is also derived from the name of a famous combat sports house in ancient Greece in Paul's days called *Palaestra*. This was a huge building that outwardly looked like a palace but it was structured for sports; more like a sports academy for boxers, wrestlers, and *pankratiasts*. This was the training place for these three types of athletes.

It is also important to know that their combat sport was very violent and deadly in those day,. You enter into the fight anticipating the worst. In fact, the fight is technically supposed to go on until one of the two surrendered or died, then the surviving one is declared a winner. There were no rules, therefore, anything goes.

You get the picture? By using the word *wrestle*, Paul, in essence, was conveying the concept that our fight against the devil is bitter, violent, and intense; anything goes as we are not supposed to be found "weak" but we must fight till the devil surrenders or we "kill" him in the right.

You fight till the end; there is no break. Likewise, our combat with the devil is an ongoing spiritual fight that we continue to engage in till our lives here on earth are over.

SATAN'S ARMY RANKS

From this scripture we are told that the devil's military's team is ranked in 4 groups:

- Principalities
- Powers
- Rulers of Darkness
- Spiritual wickedness in heavenly places

The Bible doesn't state specifically the numbers in each, but it is clear that are in an organized structured manner. While the devil and his hosts don't love each other, their strengths lie in their unity.

"Principalities" in Greek means *archas* which means rule as in "*kingly or magisterial.*"[34]

Therefore, this group are spirits who have been given the highest positions of authority in the devil's kingdom. Thus, Paul is saying that principalities in Satan's kingdom are his top group who hold the highest office in authority and power.

The second group is called, powers, from the root Greek word, *exousia* which means "*delegated authority.*"[35] Hence, this group are demon spirits who have received delegated authority from the devil to carry out his agenda.

The third group is the rulers of darkness of this world. Greek is *kosmokratór* which comes from two root words in the Greek, *kosmos* which means "*world, orderly systems.*"[36] and *krateó* which means "*to place under one's grasp or put under control.*"[37]

Therefore, *kosmokratór* means they put you under the control of the world systems. In other words, this group are world rulers responsible for influencing the worldly system and getting people to be independent of God.[38]

The fourth group are spiritual wickedness in higher places. The Greek word for wickedness is *kakia*, and it means "*malignity, malice, ill-will, desire to injure.*"[39] Therefore, this group injures, and carries out evil desires and viscous activities of the devil.

ACTIVITIES OF DEMONS

Since Satan cannot be in more than one place at a time, these are the forces he delegates to various locations. They either act alone or they congregate to oppress people. Because they are spirits without bodies, they always seek human vessels as channels through which they carry out their plans. A typical example of group demon possession was the story of the man, possessed by a legion of demons who was set free by Jesus according to Mark 5:1–20.

They Cause Physical and Mental Sickness

> "When evening came, after the sun had set, they began bringing to Him all who were ill and those who were demon-possessed...And He healed many who were ill with various diseases and cast out many demons"
>
> (MARK 1:32, 34).

One of the major activities of demons is to torment the body with sickness or disease. Most illnesses that are caused by the devil were actually carried out by demons. Also, in Mark 5, Jesus healed a man that was demon-possessed and was mentally ill as well. He could not stay with people but lived among the tombs and usually created a major disturbance in that area. The cure was not rehabilitation but to simply cast out the demon by the power of God.

They Instigate and Promote Impure Lifestyle

> "Wherein in time past ye walked according to the course of this world, according to the prince of the power of the air, the spirit that now worketh in the children of disobedience"
>
> (EPH. 2:2).

Many times, Christians struggle to take the right step or do the right thing that is pleasing to God. Most times, demons are involved in leading Christians into moral compromise. The Bible calls them the spirit of disobedience.

As I said earlier, the real enemy is the devil. But he has no authorized place on the earth to operate since he is a spirit. So, he needs a physical body as a form of space to occupy and carry out his assignment. Ephesians 4:27 (WEB) says, "*And don't give place to the devil.*"

But if you do not understand that, you will always be fighting, not knowing your stance, or taking it personally when really, people are not your enemy. Ephesians 6:12 says, "*For our wrestling is not against flesh and blood....*" Although the devil can possess people that allow him to carry out his task, it's not really about them—the real war is against the devil. In Matthew 16:23, Jesus looked at Peter and said, "*get thee behind me Satan,*" he knew the attack was not for Peter but the devil speaking through him.

Set your target correctly even as we proceed to discuss how you can really overcome.

Our Weapons of Mass Destruction

> "For the weapons of our warfare are not carnal but mighty in God for pulling down strongholds, Casting down arguments and every high thing that exalts itself against the knowledge of God, bringing every thought into captivity to the obedience of Christ, and being ready to punish all disobedience when your obedience is fulfilled"
>
> (2 COR. 10:4-6)

I guess you might be wondering why all this profound exposition about the devil? Really, I am not trying to exalt him in any way, No! or trying get you afraid to take steps towards your God-given dreams. But just like Carey Nieuwholf once said, *"the greatest mistake a Christian can make with evil is to overestimate or underestimate its influence."*[40] And Paul admonishes us not to be ignorant of oppositions against us, so we won't be deceived like Eve who thought everyone around her was for her.

You are a Winner!

> "In everything, we have won more than a victory because of Christ who loves us"
>
> (ROM. 8:37 CEV).

Understand that as Christians, we fight from the place of victory, not to victory. In all-natural battles, winners are declared at the end of the battle, but as a Christian, the battle has been declared in your favor. The victory is delivered to you already. You are not fighting to win; you have won already. Jesus has won the battle already.

The devil knows he has been defeated but still tries to pretend and disguise as though the battle is still on. and the winner is not decided, so he comes to you with different deceptive moves just to make you bow to him.

But how can you overcome all these schemes, because that is all he has now. He has nothing substantial to defeat you. However, we still need to be battle-ready. We are in a spiritual warfare. We are soldiers of Christ, so we must be dressed for victory at all times.

Defensive and Offensive Weapons

In the military, soldiers are trained and armed with armor that defends them from the enemy's attacks and as well as strategies that get the enemy down. Anyone familiar with that world is also aware when it comes to the strategic tactics, that there is the *offensive* strategy, which is to initiate violence against the enemy while a defensive strategy guards the soldier from being hurt by the devices or weapons of their enemy and also further prepared to defeat those attacks through counter violence.

Likewise, the believer has been armed by God with both defensive and offensive weapons against the devil and his demons.

DEFENSIVE WEAPON: THE WHOLE ARMOR OF GOD

> "Finally, be strong in the Lord and in the strength of his might. Put on the whole armor of God, that you may be able to stand against the wiles of the devil. For our wrestling is not against flesh and blood, but against the principalities, against the powers, against the world's rulers of the darkness of this age, and against the spiritual forces of wickedness in the heavenly places. Therefore put on the whole armor of God, that you may be able to withstand in the evil day, and, having done Stand therefore, having the utility belt of truth buckled around your waist, and having put on the breastplate of righteousness, and having fitted your feet with the preparation of the Good News of peace; above all, taking up the shield of faith, with which you will be able to quench all the fiery darts of the evil one. And take the helmet of salvation, and the sword of the Spirit, which is the word of God"
>
> (EPH. 6:10-17)

The above scripture was part of a letter written by the Apostle Paul to the Church in Ephesians. During that period, the church was grieving the Holy Spirit through their works of the flesh: behaving immaturely and not recognizing that the culprit behind all the fights, gossip, and wrong speaking was in fact the devil, who was working behind the scenes by using their character flaws and works of the flesh to his advantage. Consequently, they were being defeated due to their ignorance of how to fight and win their invisible battles.

Therefore, in addressing the issue at hand in addition to laying foundations of the church, family life, and leadership, as a father and a Roman citizen, he chose to use the final chapter to awaken the church to their warfare and also most importantly address the mighty spiritual arsenal at their disposal through Jesus Christ. Using the analogy of a Roman soldier, the soldiers of their time, he illuminated spiritual truths with the help of the Holy Spirit through their armor.

Paul admonishes that we are not in contention with physical forces but with the devil, and we must understand the weapons that are available to us if we are to remain strong in the battle of life. The weapons are for us to stand in the evil day, against the devices and schemes or wiles of the devil.

But first...

Paul cautions us to "*be strong in the Lord and in the Power of His might*" (verse 1).

When you study the Greek, the language in which this epistle was written, the imperative "be strong" is from the word *enduo* and it is used to describe *"the act of putting on a new set of clothes."*[41] For instance, when the season changes and we enter into winter, we don't wear tank tops and slippers in zero degree chilling weather, rather we put on clothes that would keep us from freezing and these clothes don't automatically come on our bodies; we take the necessary steps to put them on.

Likewise, Paul was admonishing us that if we are going to be victorious in our battles against the enemy, we must deliberately "put on" the armor of God and not to walk about the battleground naked just like we would put on warm clothes in winter. Try wearing summer clothes in serious winter conditions, and you are on your way to pneumonia and other health conditions. Likewise, walking in the enemy's camp naked, would have you defeated over and over again.

Therefore, having the power of God in our lives is the prerequisite to operating in spiritual weaponry, which is rooted in an intimate relationship with Him.

You cannot engage in effective spiritual warfare with the devil if you are already on his side through your daily lifestyle choices and decisions of the flesh. He has already conquered you. Make sure you first submit to God, which will produce power in your life, then you can put on the whole armor of God which will give you full coverage against all his schemes, tricks, and methods against you.

> "Therefore submit to God. Resist the devil and he will flee from you"
>
> (JAM. 4:7 NKJV).

Now this doesn't mean there will be times you won't fall. In fact, soldiers who go to battles get wounded from time to time but they get up and get healed and continue against their enemies.

Likewise, as a child of God, there will be times you will fall, but don't make it a habitual thing to stay in the enemy's camp, playing with him and making him defeat you by being naked through your choices. God forbids us to not make any room for the devil (Eph. 4:27).

We give him access into our lives through sin, so shut him out of your life by submitting to God. This then gives you the power to resist him, and he is supposed to flee from you. Don't try fighting the devil or putting on any armor if you know you are not in a relationship with the source of that armor; that is a recipe for disaster.

So, what then are the various outfits as highlighted from the verses above?

The Belt of Truth

For a soldier, the belt is the piece of armor to which all other pieces are held including the sword. This represents the truth of God's word. Jesus said, *"thy word is truth"* (John 17:17). The truth of the word is the foundation on which our faith stands. You must allow the word to reflect in all that you do. Hold on to it regardless of the changing culture and trends.

The Breastplate of Righteousness

In the armor of a Roman soldier, the breastplate served as protection for some of the most important parts of the body. The breastplate covers the heart, lungs, and other vital organs necessary for life. This refers to your way of life. Having known the truth of the word, it should reflect in your manner of life. Professing one thing and living another life only makes a hole on your armor for the devil to penetrate.

The Gospel of Peace

The shoe of the soldier is designed to make him go far in the journey and walk through rough terrains with confidence. The gospel of Jesus brings peace, and it should be an assurance for us that no matter where or in what condition we find ourselves, we have peace amid the storm.

The Shield of Faith

A shield helps protect a soldier from missiles thrown at him. In like manner, the devil throws negative thoughts, sin, and temptations at us. But, by faith, we can extinguish them and secure our victory. Our hope in God helps us overlook any attraction from the devil unto God.

The Helmet of Salvation

Helmets helps to protect against any injury to the head, which can be life-threatening. As believers we need to guard our lives and secure our faith in God. Salvation further gives us an assurance that the victory is sure in Christ.

Sword of the Spirit

Apart from weapons to defend ourselves, we also have weapons to fight and engage in battle. One of them is the word of God also known as the Sword of the Spirit. We must be equipped with scriptures to shut the devil up and bring down negative imaginations. In Matthew 4, Jesus won the battle with the devil when he was tempted by the word. So, study the word and trust the Holy Spirit to remind you when you need it.

OFFENSIVE WEAPONS

> "Behold, I give you the authority to trample on serpents and scorpions, and over all the power of the enemy, and nothing shall by any means hurt you"

(LUKE 10:19).

God has given us weapons of authority where we also attack the devil directly. These are what is known in the military as offensive weapons.

1. The blood of Jesus.
2. The words of our testimony.
3. Praise.
4. The name of Jesus.
5. Holy Lifestyle.
6. Obedience to God
7. Fasting and Prayers.

Plead the Blood

"And they overcame him by the blood of the Lamb"

(REV. 12:11)

Jesus conquered the devil when He shed His blood on the cross. That's the ultimate defeat and today the blood of Jesus is speaking better things on our behalf (Heb. 12:24). When you apply the blood of Jesus over yourself and everything around you, you have conquered the devil.

Testify of His Goodness

> "I will bless the Lord at all times and his praise will continually be in my mouth"
>
> (PS. 34:1 NKJV).

Praises not only break bondages but also bring deliverance to all those around us during the praises. When the prisoners heard the praises of Paul and Silas, they were also set free because they were in the same environment with them (Acts 16). Your praise is a weapon against the enemy. When you share what God has done for you, either through music or speaking, it becomes a weapon against all your enemies.

Mention the Name of Jesus

> "[T]hat at the name of Jesus every knee should bow, of those in heaven, and of those on earth, and of those under the earth, and that every tongue should confess that Jesus Christ is Lord, to the glory of God the Father"
>
> (PHIL. 2:10–11 NKJV).

The name Jesus carries a heavy weight in the spirit. Actually, it is a law that once it is mentioned, every knee must bow including the devil and his demons. So, mention it every chance you get. This mighty name gives you access and favor with your Heavenly Father and also cripples the devils.

Stay Connected with God Through Prayers & Fasting

Just as we can't live without air, a Christian cannot live without prayer. Prayer is simply communicating with God. Throughout the Bible, we are commanded to incorporate our prayers with fasting. This is because fasting is intentionally denying the flesh in order to pave way for the spirit to take mastery of us. When you deny the flesh of its gratification through fasting and prayers, you get more results in life and you also get clarity in hearing God and living victoriously for God. Check out this scripture:

> "Is this not the fast that I have chosen: To loose the bonds of wickedness, To undo the [a]heavy burdens, To let the oppressed go free, And that you break every yoke?"

(ISA. 58:6 NKJV).

There are certain bondages that won't suddenly leave until you have fasted and prayed. So, while prayer paves the way, use the weapon of fasting to break yokes and remove any burden so you can enjoy a victorious life.

Live to Please God

> "Therefore submit to God. Resist the devil and he will flee from you"

(JAMES 4:7 NKJV).

As already mentioned, when you abstain from evil ways and you live to please only the Lord, you naturally put a hedge of protection around your life that keeps you safe.

Finally...

Resist the devil at all times with boldness and confidence, and he will flee after you have submitted to God through obedience.

No matter what the attack against you may look like, you have all it takes to overcome. You are not a victim but a victor. Also, pray always. When the devil tried Peter, Jesus had to pray for him so he can stand.

Remember, Proverbs 24:10 (ESV) says, *"If you faint in the day of adversity, your strength is small."* So take responsibility, equip yourself, and don't give up. If you fall, stand up again. Your dream is too precious, don't give in to discouragement, you have all the help you need in the person of the Holy Spirit. So, I believe you can. And you will,

See you at the medals stand.

KEY TAKEAWAY : You have an enemy who works tirelessly to stop you from fulfilling your destiny. On the other hand, God is with you. He has also given you mighty weapons and armor to fight back and establish your victory through Jesus Christ.

DANCE TO THE BEAT OF YOUR DREAMS

SECTION V

Unstopping #YourYes

Welcome to the last section. This is your personal invitation to accept the clarion call of God to step into your greatness with fearless confidence, what I sometimes call as GOD-fidence. In this section, you will discover how to break free from self-sabotage, heal from every traumatic experience from your past and step into what could be your best life yet in God.

13

Your Passport to Possibilities

"Behold the maidservant of the Lord! Let it be to me according to your word"

(LUKE 1: 38 NKJV).

It will cost you everything to obey the divine calling of God for your life! Mary risked losing her marriage, her fiancé and also her own life and dream to pursue God's dream for her.

Mind you, when the angel came, he didn't mention anything about Joseph and it's also interesting to note that Mary too didn't ask about Joseph; she was more concerned about doing the Will of God for her life without counting the cost of the risks involved. From her current standpoint, there was no guarantee of marriage. Hence, saying yes to God would mean a life of shame and disgrace to her and her family, and put her own life at risk, marriage loss and all the other things that were involved. This was a very dangerous and risky business.

Why would a God of Love put a young girl's life in jeopardy? That is what many of us would say the least but God knew what

He was doing. I have the same question for you today: what are you willing to lose in order to do the assignment of God for your life? Is it your spouse? A good reputation? Money? Family? Company? Education?

Bye, Felicia

In 1995, a comedy movie, called *Friday* was released. In the movie, a phrase which has transcended that generation to ours was made by a lead actor, Ice Cube. During the movie scene, a lady passing by asked for something specific from two men who were sitting by their door post, and in his refusal to her request, Ice Cube dismissed her by saying "Bye, Felicia!"

The phrase "Bye, Felicia" according to Ice Cube, is "the phrase 'to get anyone out of your face'," and, as it was used in the movie scene, it is generally intended as a dismissive kiss-off. Two decades later, since the release of the movie, this phrase has become very popular as it is commonly used to dismiss things, situations, or individuals that we longer want to associate ourselves with or tolerate.[42]

Well, before the concept of this movie was ever produced, thousands of years ago, an apostle of the Lord wrote his own dismissive kiss-off. Penned in his letter to the Philippian church, let's read together:

> "Brethren, I do not count myself to have apprehended; but one thing I do, FORGETTING THOSE THINGS WHICH ARE ARE BEHIND, and reaching forward to those things which are ahead,, I press toward the goal for the prize of the upward call of God in Christ Jesus"
>
> (PHIL. 3:14, EMPHASIS ADDED).

Many of us celebrate the Apostle Paul for his great accomplishment in standing for Christ and writing two thirds of the New Testament but what many fail to realize is that he also had an ugly past: he was a murderer who was also saved by Grace!

Before he became Paul, He was Saul—a name that I am sure he fought so hard to forget due to the past memories it brought. You must realize that name came with bad record of killing many innocent lives until his encounter with Jesus Christ, while sojourning to Damascus, a journey which was serving a similar purpose of killing and arresting more lives.

In his day, those who believed in Jesus were considered blasphemers of the true gospel of the Mosaic Torah. As we just read, Paul starts out the second part of this verse with the words *"but one thing I do."* And then from there he goes into the revelation of not looking at what was behind him, but pressing forward for those things which now ahead of him.

The words *"but one thing I do"* are put in the context of something that he is really making sure that he does on a regular and consistent basis. Of course he knew fully well the wrong things he did but he was now putting in a deliberate effort that would require self-discipline not to let his past experiences and mistakes hinder him from experiencing the present and future rewards installed for him or worst be punished by them on a continual basis.

To Paul, it was definitely a *Bye, Felicia!*, his own dismissive kick-off which he was so much intentional about as he pursued the calling on his life.

Because, he understood first hand, that it was very easy to start falling back on all of the bad things that may have occurred in his past, and then use that as an excuse to start feeling sorry for himself, throw a pity party or to justify some of the irrational things which might have crossed his mind or worst, respond to the label by people who knew his past wrongs could have placed on him because people are usually unforgiving for past sins or mistakes. Hence, Bye Felicia!

Likewise, one of the things that tend to cripple us on our obedience to God's assignments for our lives is the shadow of our past mistakes. It tends to frighten us especially when we are ready to step out, because we suddenly become aware of them. But the reality is that, all of us have a certain amount of baggage that we carry from our past. Due to the fallen nature of this world, we are all stuck having to deal with the harsh reality of pure evil in our lives through the activities of demonic spirits and people who have chosen with their own free will to live this life out on the dark side. Every minute of every day someone is getting murdered, robbed, abused, or abducted. We literally cannot go one day without some kind of this activity being reported on our local news channels.

Consequently, all of us get or will get hurt one way or another in this life. And some of these hurts end up being extreme and traumatic for many of us that we are not able to easily let it slide.

While some are able to carry lighter loads, the majority of us, on the other hand, have not managed to break free from our past; we are still mired down in the hurts and injustices and cannot seem to get any victory over any of it— either in our thinking or emotions.

Therefore, we find ourselves rehearsing these wounds in our lives in unending cycles, which manifest themselves in diverse ways and bondages including unhealthy soul ties, addictions, abuse, low self-esteem/self-hatred, anger etc. that will require the power of the Holy Spirit to break free.

Nonetheless, we can be free, if we will allow God the room to work on us because regardless of our past experiences, we are still not our mistakes; neither do our experiences define us. We can let God use those mistakes, experiences and trauma to help transform us into better people and the lessons learned to help others too in their own life journey and walk with God; it is never God's intentions that our experiences will deter us from the future He has in store for us but rather they will work together for our good as we pursue His Purpose for our lives (Rom. 8:28).

Surrender All

Growing up, I was very athletic and an avid sports lover. Anyone who knew me from childhood would attest to the fact that I loved to play soccer, volleyball, tennis, and swimming and I even recall how I used to proudly wear my #3 soccer jersey for my school team.

Fast forward, the journey of adulthood began and like many of you, I lost myself in that process of becoming. Therefore, as time went by, I decided to revived my athletic self again by first improving on my swimming skills. Thus, enrolling in swimming lessons.

As the lessons began, it didn't take long for me to rediscover that the art and skill of swimming is actually based on a very simple concept: Trust the Water, Let Go and You Will Float; Resist & You Will Drown.

Despite the simplicity of this concept, it is also the most difficult thing to do but without learning to surrender, you are not going to float which will also mean you will not be able to swim!

THE ART OF SURRENDER : A CHILDLIKE APPROACH

The dictionary defines surrender as *"putting one's full weight on someone or something."*[43] It involves letting go- a release of effort, tension and fear. And it involves trust. You cannot let go of self-dependence and transfer dependence on someone without trust. And when it comes to swimming, it is either you learn to trust the water to hold you or forget about floating.

That was a rude awakening for me because I remember, as a little girl this was no issue, but now that I am an adult, being so self-dependent, it was not that easy to fully let myself go and "trust" this pool to keep me afloat without having to do anything, something we, adults are not usually wired for; we are used to doing things and working hard to get results, anything that involves relaxing to get the same result does not make sense to our rational mind.

This got me thinking about the power of surrender in our relationship with God; walking with God is like learning how to swim. You do not know the adventure that awaits you until you are in the water and while it might be scary at first, it is also the most liberating and fulfilling experience anyone can have.

BRACE YOURSELF FOR THE ADVENTURE THAT AWAITS YOU!

A lot of us assume that just because God gave us that commission things would be easy. Well, honey, I beg to differ! I'm here to break down all your assumptions about God! He not only tries us but sometimes also, He grabs us at the height of what we consider our apex or the climax of our life progression.

Have you ever been in a situation when you were on the verge of that promotion and you sense the Lord to leave and start your own business or volunteer for a job etc.

This was what happened to me personally. In my Junior year in college, I sensed the calling of God for me to drop out of college temporary to respond to the call. While it was not convenient, I also knew in my heart that was God nudging me to do it. Now while it didn't make sense to anyone, even to me, I had this boldness and inner piece that assured me that everything was going to be alright even though I didn't have a definite plan back then.

Now looking back, I'm so glad I said yes to God, even though the next several years was going to try my faith and test my obedience because the lessons I learned and who I became in that process is what has birthed this book today. Now it has given me more confidence to keep jumping to the next assignments He aligns on my path because I know of a surety that He is always with me and will enable me make them all happen; those experiences stay with you permanently.

You must realize that just because you respond to the assignment does not automatically mean everything will be rosy and it will be a smooth ride but you can be rest assured that God is with you every step of the way and will guide your steps as you progress.

You might be in a dilemma, trying to stay safe, But the Choice Is All Yours!

PRAYER OF COMPLETE SURRENDER

What an adventure, isn't it? But wait a minute; have you discovered your God-given dream(s) and vision(s) yet? Are you struggling with thoughts to pursue them? Maybe you have been delaying because of fear and uncertainties. Fear of the unknown or what people will say. Are you scared of failing, or they look too big in your eyes to accomplish? If your answer is Yes to any of the aforementioned questions, I'd like you to say this simple prayer of faith with me in surrender to the Holy Spirit, who is your Greatest Helper:

My Heavenly Father, I admit I have doubts in my heart, but today I surrender my all to You. I believe You have not given me the spirit of fear, but of power, therefore I receive the power to pursue and fulfill this vision you have given me.

You said in Your word that apart from You, I can do nothing; therefore, I lay down my might and ability, and I rest on Your grace that makes the journey easy. I no longer struggle with You, but instead, I cooperate with Your Spirit to conceive and birth Your purpose for my life.

For all that You have placed on my heart Lord, I declare that they will be done by the leading of the Holy Spirit. I refuse to grow weary or discouraged anymore. I shall accomplish all that I'm destined to be. In Jesus Name. Amen!

KEY TAKEAWAY: You are only one decision away from living out all the awesome plans and purpose God has for you. All you need to do is to embrace them and surrender to the Holy Spirit so He can do awesome things with you that will glorify God. Your yes is the passport to your greatness. Use it!

Knowing Jesus Intimately

You have come to the end of this book. But just before you drop it. As you already know the journey of a thousand miles begins with a step, so also the journey to your fulfillment of divine plan begins by first giving your life to Jesus. Without whom, you can't even receive the help to fulfill His purpose for your life and you definitely will remain stranded.

You see, every human being has a dream, goal or desire in their heart but the difference between Christians and unbelievers is the Presence of God and the guarantee of eternity with God afterwards. The life we are currently living, in actual fact is a dress rehearsal for eternity. What you do now actually matters and if you don't know God as your Heavenly Father intimately, everything you are doing now, while it may be worthwhile, ends with you when you die.

However, should you become of His family, everything you're doing here on earth, including the dreams and visions you are realizing, follows with you into eternity and guess what: you get to be rewarded for your service.

So my question to you now is: do you know Jesus intimately? If the answer is a No, an unsure yes or both, then here is your chance to get to know Him; He is only a prayer away. Just say this simple prayer with all sincerely from your heart and by faith:

> *Lord Jesus, I admit that I am a sinner, and I cannot save myself. And I believe you died for me. Right now, I repent of all my sins and shortcomings. Forgive me, wash me, and cleanse me with your blood.*

From today, I renounce the devil and his works in my life. And I declare that by grace, I am now a child of God, I am now the righteousness of God in Christ Jesus. Come into my heart Lord Jesus and be my Savior. Thank you, Jesus, for saving me. In Jesus name. Amen.

Hurray, if you said the above prayer, welcome to God's family! I'd urge you to find a Bible believing church in your area to attend. If you need help, they are around you. Start with browsing online. Use google, mobile apps and YouTube to get resources to help you grow. Also, you need to ask for help from matured Christians to help you get started on your new journey with Christ.

You may also reach out to our outreach ministry to help you get started. Send us an email at saved@meetjesus.life and a minister of God will reach out to you.

Work with Me

If you need help realizing your dreams and visions, or perhaps you need help, a cheerleader to hold you accountable to guide you every step of the way and to also help you clarify your visions and set actionable goals to materialize them, then I'm here for you!

As a Certified Christian Life Coach with over ten years of experience, I'm poised to serve you. Through my systematic and hands-on approach to coaching, I will help you to move from the dream stage to the achievable results that will have you winning by God's grace. Visit my website to join any of my programs and let's get started : www.destinyunplugged.com

For other inquiries including speaking engagements, ministerial partnerships, endorsements, bulk orders etc, visit my website at www.feliciaasomaning.com

God bless you!

Meet the Author

Felicia Asomaning is a multi-talented woman of God with a mandate to stir people up for true revival, awaken them into their divine destiny and equip them to live out their best lives. She is also the Founding Pastor of Church Unplugged Inc., mentor, entrepreneur, psalmist, life coach, nutritionist, speaker and networker. Her driving passion for unity in the Body of Christ motivates her to network various ministries and organizations for a common goal and exponential results. She has become a hub that fosters various relationships across ethnicity, cultures, and denomination. For more information, visit feliciaasomaning.com

End Notes

1. Pope John XXIII Quotes. BrainyQuote.com, BrainyMedia Inc, 2019. https://www.brainyquote.com/quotes/pope_john_xxiii_109443, accessed July 4, 2019.
2. Brandon Harrison Quotes. BrainyQuote.com, BrainyMedia Inc, 2020. https://www.brainyquote.com/quotes/brandon_harrison_389852, accessed August 13, 2020.
3. Charles R. Swindoll Quotes. BrainyQuote.com, BrainyMedia Inc, 2020. https://www.brainyquote.com/quotes/charles_r_swindoll_388332, accessed August 13, 2020.
4. "Martha Stewart and Her Incredible Comeback." 2010. Oprah.Com. Oprah.com. October 5, 2010. https://www.oprah.com/oprahshow/martha-stewart-and-her-incredible-comeback.
5. "Facebook." n.d. Facebook.Com. Accessed August 14, 2021. https://m.facebook.com/story.php?story_fbid=10164584716415447&substory_index=0&id=91383850446.
6. Strand, Robert. *Moments for Grandparents*. New Leaf Press, 1995.
7. Oxford Online Dictionary, s.v. "mandate," accessed November 20, 2019, https://www.lexico.com/en/definition/mandate.
8. "Treasure in CLAY Object Lesson & Story." *CreativeBibleStudy.com*, www.creativebiblestudy.com/treasure-in-clay.html.
9. Chestnut, Stephen. "Legacy." 20 Nov. 2020.
10. BarackObama. " Raw Video: Barack Obama's 2008 acceptance

speech," Youtube Video, 18:10, November 6, 2012. https://www.youtube.com/ watch?v=LE07lzfpdCU

11. Word Hippo, s.v. "phantasia," accessed November 20, 2019, https:// biblehub.com/greek/5325
12. Bible Study Notes. Accessed on August 8, 2020. https://www.biblestudynote.com/blog/what-is-the-difference-between-logos-and-rhema/
13. Institute in Basic Life Principles. Accessed on August 9, 2020. https://iblp.org/questions/what-rhema
14. Munroe, Myles. In Pursuit of Purpose: the Legacy and Wisdom of Myles Munroe. Destiny Image Pub, 1992.
15. Keith Rosen, M. C. C. 2017. "The Power of Why – A King's Fable and Lesson in Leadership by Keith Rosen." Keithrosen.Com. February 5, 2017. https://keithrosen.com/2017/02/the-power-of-why-a-kings-fable-and-lesson-in-leadership/.
16. Myles Munroe. "Dr. Myles Munroe – 25 Life Lessons from Incarnation Part 2," YouTube Video, 4:13, January 2, 2010, https://www.youtube. com/watch?v=YAywpRpXgAk
17. Merriam Webster Online Dictionary, s.v. "virgin," accessed October 18, 2019, https://www.merriam-webster.com/dictionary/virgin.
18. Cambridge Online Dictionary, s.v. "instinct," accessed July 25, 2019, https://dictionary.cambridge.org/us/dictionary/english/instinct.
19. Word Hippo, s.v. "providentia," accessed December 10, 2019, https:// www.wordhippo.com/what-is/the-meaning-of/latin-word-8169dbb 234a22a417fab6c36c97385a61c591cbd.html.
20. Encyclopedia Mythica, s.v. "providentia," accessed November 9, 2019, https://pantheon.org/articles/p/providentia.html.
21. Strong's Exhaustive Concordance, s.v., "raah," accessed February 15, 2020, https://biblehub.com/hebrew/7200.htm.

22. Mission: Impossible: The 6 Movie Collection, directed by Bruce Geller, Brian De Palma, John Woo, J.J. Abrams, Brad Bird, and Christopher McQuarrie (1996; Paramount Pictures, 2018), Blu-Ray.
23. SteveHarvey. "Steve Harvey | Faith Makes It Possible," YouTube Video, 3:27, April 28, 2019, https://www.youtube.com/ watch?v=-BCJwG7xrz4
24. SteveHarvey. "Steve Harvey | My Anchor," YouTube Video, 4:37, November 28, 2020, https://www.youtube.com/watch?v=bxLe1DutJWA
25. Merriam Webster Online Dictionary, s.v. "mentor," accessed October 18, 2019, https://www.merriam-webster.com/dictionary/mentor.
26. Lexico Online Dictionary. "train," accessed October 18, 2019, https:// www.lexico.com/en/definition/train
27. John Wesley Quotes. BrainyQuote.com, BrainyMedia Inc, 2019. https://www.brainyquote.com/quotes/john_wesley_524892, accessed September 4, 2019
28. Tim Sanders Quotes. goodreads.com, Goodreads Inc, 2019. https:// www.goodreads.com/quotes/851957-your-network-is-your-networth, accessed September 4, 2019.
29. "Definition of RECEPTOR." n.d. Merriam-Webster.Com. Accessed August 15, 2019. https://www.merriam-webster.com/dictionary/receptor.
30. "Definition of RECEPTOR." n.d. Merriam-Webster.Com. Accessed August 15, 2019. https://www.merriam-webster.com/dictionary/receptor.
31. "Definition of HONOR." n.d. Merriam-Webster.Com. Accessed August 15, 2021. https://www.merriam-webster.com/dictionary/honor?utm_campaign=sd&utm_medium=serp&utm_source=jsonld.
32. "Definition of ORDERED." n.d. Merriam-Webster.Com. Ac-

cessed August 15, 2021. https://www.merriam-webster.com/dictionary/ordered.
33. Strong's Exhaustive Concordance, s.v. "palé," accessed February 15, 2020, https://biblehub.com/greek/3823.htm.
34. Strong's Exhaustive Concordance, s.v. "archas," accessed February 15, 2020, https://biblehub.com/greek/746.htm.
35. Strong's Exhaustive Concordance, s.v., "exousia," accessed February 15, 2020, https://biblehub.com/greek/1849.htm.
36. Strong's Exhaustive Concordance, s.v. "kosmos," accessed February 15, 2020, https://biblehub.com/greek/2889.htm.
37. Strong's Exhaustive Concordance, s.v. "krateó," accessed February 15, 2020, https://biblehub.com/greek/2902.htm.
38. Strong's Exhaustive Concordance, s.v. "kosmokratór," accessed February 15, 2020, https://biblehub.com/str/greek/2888.htm.
39. Strong's Exhaustive Concordance, "kakia," accessed February 15, 2020, https://biblehub.com/str/greek/2549.htm.
40. Nieuwholf, Carey. "The Devil's 5 Favorite Strategies : Church Leader Edition" (blog) Accessed November 19, 2019. https://careynieuwhof. com/the-devils-5-favourite-strategies-church-leader-edition/
41. Strong's Exhaustive Concordance, "enduo," accessed February 15, 2020, https://biblehub.com/str/greek/2549.htm.
42. "Bye, Felicia," Friday, directed by Ice Cube, DJ Pooh, and F. Gary Gray (1995; Burbank, CA: New Line Productions, Ghetto Bird Productions), meme, https://en.wikipedia.org/wiki/ Friday_(1995_film).
43. Merriam Webster Online Dictionary, s.v. "surrender," accessed January 18, 2020, https://www.merriam-webster.com/dictionary/surrender

www.ingramcontent.com/pod-product-compliance
Lightning Source LLC
Chambersburg PA
CBHW022041200426
43209CB00072B/1917/J